METAPHYSICS

*the text of this book is printed
on 100% recycled paper*

By the Same Author

METAPHYSICS

AN INTRODUCTION

ARCHIE J. BAHM

Professor of Philosophy
University of New Mexico

BARNES & NOBLE BOOKS

A DIVISION OF HARPER & ROW, PUBLISHERS

New York, Evanston, San Francisco, London

First BARNES & NOBLE BOOKS edition published 1974

LIBRARY OF CONGRESS CATALOG CARD NUMBER: 73-7469

STANDARD BOOK NUMBER: 06-463338-1

CONTENTS

PART THREE: DIALECTIC

ACKNOWLEDGMENTS

I wish to acknowledge with gratitude permission to republish much of "A Multiple-Aspect Theory of Time" from the *Southwestern Journal of Philosophy* 2 (Spring–Summer 1971): 163–171, as part of chapter 11, and of "Wholes and Parts" from the *Southwestern Journal of Philosophy* 3 (Spring 1972): 17–22, as part of chapter 10.

INTRODUCTION

1 / WHY METAPHYSICS?

Every thinking person, sooner or later, asks himself the questions: What am I? Why am I here? How did I get here? What is my future? These questions inevitably give rise to other questions about the nature of existence, of both self and the world.

Some persons raise these questions without help from others. Some become aroused by hearing others discuss them. Since mankind has been troubled by such questions for a very long time, a vast literature has accumulated. As curiosity continues, the problems become more complicated, so much so that we now divide them into groups, sometimes called *sciences*. The division of questions about matter, life, and society into the physical, biological, and social sciences is well known. Each group, each science, and each subscience has its own primary problems.

Other, more general questions, have been reserved for the philosophical sciences, often divided for convenience into three groups: those inquiring into the nature of existence, called *metaphysics;* those inquiring into the nature of knowledge, called *epistemology;* and those inquiring into the nature of values, called *axiology.* Each of these has its more particular sciences and subsciences. Axiology, for example, includes questions about the nature of beauty and ugliness, constituting *aesthetics* as a science; right and wrong, constituting *ethics* as a science; and religion, the investigation of which is called *philosophy of religion.*

The questions constituting metaphysics are among the most general that can be asked. And answers to these questions are needed before we can expect to find satisfactory answers to our more specific questions. For whether we are aware of this fact or not, questions and answers of this most general sort are presupposed when we ask questions and seek more specific answers. That is, matter, life, and society, the subjects investigated by the physical, biological, and social sciences, exist. Now if there are some characteristics common to all existences, then those characteristics are common also to all that is material, all that is alive, and all that is social. Hence the physical, biological, and social sciences do not escape metaphysical problems but presuppose their solution. If doubts remain about solutions to these problems, then they remain as doubts affecting the solutions to all other sciences. (The same is true of epistemological problems and their solutions; for if "science" is, or involves, "knowledge," then any residue of uncertainty regarding the nature of knowledge in general functions also as uncertainty regarding the nature of particular kinds of knowledge that may be claimed by physicists, biologists, or sociologists.)

Hence the importance of metaphysical inquiry, both for personal satisfaction and for scientific advancement, should not be underestimated. Persons achieving competence in metaphysics have acquired a competence that will help them in dealing with problems in all other fields. If one can arrive at satisfactory answers to metaphysical questions, he will have answers to apply to all other questions that can be asked about existing things. Even if one merely becomes acquainted with the problems and the typical difficulties inherent in dealing with them, without achieving satisfactory answers, he thereby becomes alerted to typical difficulties inherent in all problems about things that exist. Reliable answers to metaphysical questions are more powerful, in the sense of being answers needed also in fully answering more specific questions, than equally reliable answers in more specific sciences.

Since many misconceive "science" as certain and "philosophy" as uncertain, some may need a reminder that a science is, first of all, an inquiry into a problem and, second, an inquiry approached with an open mind. The history of science is a history of trials and errors; many more hypotheses are abondoned than retained after being tried. "Progress in science" means that previously held scientific theories have been replaced by more adequate theories. The research scientist, who differs from many "Chemistry I lab instructors," does not have a closed mind with pat answers but devotes himself to speculative exploration of unanswered questions. That more satisfactory answers have been achieved at some times than at others, and in some fields than in others, is obvious. But the popular mistaken notion, that science consists of solved problems and philosophy of unsolved or even unsolvable problems, overlooks the fact that answers to philosophical problems are presupposed by every answer to any other scientific problem and that ignorance of that fact does not eliminate it. If our metaphysical questions remain unanswered, then supposed answers to our questions in other areas are not so fully and finally answered as we may suppose. Part of the purpose of an introduction to metaphysical inquiry is to dispel some illusions of certainty regarding answers to some other scientific problems and to provide more powerful insights into what is needed for fuller solutions to all problems.

2 / WHAT IS METAPHYSICS?

Metaphysics begins as an *inquiry into existence*. For those who discover, or believe, that existence has a "nature," that is, some general characteristics, metaphysics becomes an *inquiry into the nature of existence*. As inquiry proceeds and attention is focused more and more on these general characteristics, then the question arises, "Which of these seemingly general characteristics are actually universal?" Then metaphysics tends to become an *inquiry into the universal characteristics of existence*. Just as each science tends to adopt terms to serve its needs more conveniently, so in metaphysics as a field of inquiry the term "category" has come to be adopted. Any characteristic that is completely universal is called "a category." One may also use the term "category" in specialized areas. For example, if a zoologist studying robins concludes that all robins have reddish colored feathers on their breasts, he may properly assert that such a universal characteristic is a category of robinhood. But in order to be a metaphysical category, a characteristic must be such that it is present in everything that exists. Given this technical language, metaphysics becomes an *inquiry into existence and its categories*.

Is metaphysics a science? For those who believe that a science is something with a fixed and final stock of certainties, the answer will be no. But for those who regard a science as a field of inquiry where research is conducted with certain attitudes and methods, metaphysics is, or certainly can be, a science. Fully conceived, a science involves six characteristics: problems, attitude, method, activity, solutions, and effects. Without a problem there can be no science; and the more difficult the problems, the more unlikely

6

that satisfactory solutions will be reached easily. The scientific attitude involves curiosity, willingness to investigate, open-mindedness about what will be found, willingness to suspend conviction until all the evidence is acquired, and persistence in the face of apparently insurmountable obstacles. Although each type of problem usually will call for a method somewhat peculiarly suited to it, philosophers of science have discovered that understanding the problem, observing relevant data, formulating hypotheses, and testing in these various ways are common methodological elements in all sciences.

The activity of researching scientists is fundamental to what constitutes science; and the advancement of scientific knowledge depends on the ability, skills, efforts, and moral conscientiousness prevailing in such research. Conclusions, in the form of hypotheses or theories, stated as general principles or laws of behavior, are desired. When they are not immediately forthcoming, "working hypotheses," or tentative solutions, are postulated and experimented with. When hypotheses repeatedly pass the tests put to them, they tend to be regarded as reliable. Whereas popular impatience leads to regarding them as "facts" and treating them as dogmas, a true scientist maintains an open mind about the possibility of new and counter evidence. Since tentativity regarding conclusions is essential to the scientific attitude, one who has become so sure of his conclusions that he has abandoned this attitude is no longer properly called "a scientist." Finally a part of what a science is consists of the effects it has on the lives of people; if "a thing is what a thing does," and if people behave differently because they believe and act on conclusions proposed by scientists, such differences are practical consequences of such science. Given the foregoing conception of science, then, metaphysics is that *science which inquires into the nature of existence and its categories.*

What has happened to our person who asks himself the question, "What am I?" He is our metaphysician. That is, everyone who inquires into the nature of himself and the universe, seeking answers of a most general sort, already is a metaphysician, provided his query is not merely an idle curiosity but is a vital challenge that he pursues earnestly and with an open mind. Persons who feel incapable, or who are too busily occupied with other affairs, may not pursue their questions very far. They do not remain metaphysical very long. But those gripped by the challenge of wanting to know what they are cannot avoid becoming more and more metaphysical. Whether they quest by themselves or seek other help, such as teachers or books, each person's quest is his own. Some complain that metaphysical problems never achieve commonly accepted solutions because such problems, like eating, loving, and reproducing, are problems each person wants to solve for himself. No matter how many other people have agreed that a certain food tastes good, each person wants to judge for himself by tasting before he consents to agreement. So also, no matter how many people have agreed that they are sons of God, manifestations of Brahman, matter in motion, or libido frustrated, each person who deeply wonders about himself wants to think his own thoughts before he assents to the opinions of others. Every metaphysical quest is personal. All such personal quests are parts of metaphysics.

3 / WHAT ARE THE CATEGORIES?

There is no way to predict what characteristic will first suggest itself to a person beginning his inquiry into the nature of existence. He may hit upon something trivial. Most likely it will turn out not to be something actually universal. Each person suggests answers in terms of his own experience. Primitive man pictured his universe in terms of ideas that we have come to call "myths." Many moderns favor stating universals in terms of mathematical formulae. In any case, those characteristics first proposed by whatever manner function as categories for such persons. And they are properly called "scientific" as long as one proposes them with an open mind and persists in his quest for evidence to test their adequacy.

If a person is educated in some group, he tends to be indoctrinated by the ideas already acceptable to that group. Its categories become his, unless doubts arise in him. And even when they do, his own ideas tend to be conditioned by the very ideas he doubts. When one is influenced by a wider society, he usually finds many other schools of thought with their own proposals about categories. If one systematically studies the histories of Western and Asian philosophy, he finds a plethora of suggestions, some of which conflict with others. Those who are impatient with their inherited traditions often hope to find greater wisdom in some foreign culture and may do so. Some merely exchange the doctrines of one cult for another, sometimes becoming happier, even if in fact no wiser.

But many persistent searchers discover that the farther they search the more convinced they become that they cannot find satisfactory ready-made solutions anywhere; they must make up their minds for themselves. For such people, the search for satisfactory answers may become a lifelong quest. Such people appreciate the following answer to the question, "What is man?" Man is a being that asks the question, "What is man?" and spends his lifetime searching for an answer.

When one discovers a trait that seems to him to be universal, he is likely to try out his proposal on others. One feels more secure in his own beliefs when he finds others who share his assurance. He thereby tends to become a sectarian indoctrinator, even if quite unwittingly. But one should seek such assurance, if he can. Indeed, a widely held criterion of scientific method is that a hypothesis cannot be regarded as scientific unless it can be communicated and tests about it can be repeated by others.

In selecting some proposed categories for examination in this volume, I am faced with the problem of choosing, not just for myself, but for others. Knowing how much people disagree about so many things, I find the task risky. I have picked, from many more that have been put forth, a limited number of terms, all but two of which occur commonly in ordinary language and receive almost daily usage by active minds. Even if the reader himself disagrees with my selection, he may recognize it as an example of metaphysical endeavor. I expect disagreement from many who have already made up their minds in other ways. But I also believe that each beginner will find both the traits proposed and the treatment of them illustrative of the kinds of answers which he may expect of metaphysicians or of himself as he pursues his own metaphysical quest.

Change, time, cause, wholes, process, purpose, action, space, substance, relations, universals, and intelligence—all are common terms that I propose to explore as categories of existence. To these I add one more, dialectic, to entice the beginner into some of the more intricate problems which sooner or later every persistent metaphysician tends to encounter. One may accept all these terms as representing characteristics of some of the things which he experiences without regarding them as categories of existence. The proposal that they are present as characteristics of every existent extends beyond what many will be willing to accept.

Furthermore, another feature of my own way of understanding existence, which some will find most natural and others very peculiar, is that these characteristics tend to occur as pairs. That is, each proposed characteristic tends to have an opposite, which also may be a category of existence. By proposing that categories occur in pairs, I am able to show, and to sharpen, issues that have been debated for centuries. This method also helps me to portray another, more complex characteristic of existence, namely, "polarity"; as my conclusions begin to take shape, polarity itself, as a kind of relation between other characteristics, now appears to me to be a category of existence. Hence as discussion proceeds, the problems will become those of change versus permanence, events versus durations, wholes versus parts, aims versus goal, agency versus patiency, and particulars versus universals.

4 / SOME DISPUTES ABOUT CATEGORIES

Although a craftier author might ignore these disputes and either hide from them permanently or leave the reader to discover them for himself, I cannot refrain from calling attention to typical criticisms that have been, and are likely to be, raised against metaphysical inquiries.

First, some deny categories of existence; but this claim daunts only the inexperienced. For implicit in it is the claim that freedom from categories is itself a category of existence. Persons who explain that no characteristic can be universal because existence is always changing are really claiming that change itself is a category of existence. If such persons insist that there can be no universals because each thing is unique, one may observe that they are insisting that uniqueness itself is a category of existence. The point here is that, if anyone is willing to enter into a dispute about metaphysics, he himself automatically becomes a metaphysician. Any denial about what characterizes all existence itself entails an assertion that all existence is characterized by the absence of such a universal.

Second, some say that even if there were any universal characteristics of existence, we could not know them. Human knowledge is limited, and there is more existence than one person, or even all the persons who ever live, can know. This statement is correct, provided we mean by "knowledge" complete comprehension, complete induction, or reproduction of all of existence within our knowledge of it. But if this is what we mean by "knowledge," few of us will ever know anything very much. In this sense, we can "know" only what appears to us. Most scientific hypotheses are stated in terms of probabilities; the more statistically refined ones are expressed also in terms of "probable error." And most personal "knowledge" claims are really "beliefs," views that we have learned to trust even in the absence of tests that might somehow assure us of their "certainty."

The challenge raised by the foregoing criticism cannot be satisfactorily met until we have completed another kind of inquiry: namely, an inquiry into the nature of experience, which has come to be called "theory of knowledge" or, more technically, "epistemology." The issues raised here are equally as difficult to deal with as those in metaphysics. And we shall arbitrarily refrain from complicating our present inquiry by attending to them also. [My experience as a teacher reveals that students, unvaryingly, when taking a course in metaphysics want to deal with problems of knowledge first and when taking a course in theory of knowledge want to deal with questions of existence first. Many books on metaphysics turn out to be treatises on theory of knowledge, and some works purporting to be about theory of knowledge are devoted primarily to speculations about the nature of existence. Hence my own resolve to focus on metaphysics here and to expand on problems of knowledge in a separate work is somewhat unusual.]

One result of such refraining is an inability to reply convincingly to the foregoing criticism here. I can only point out that proposals about universal characteristics of existence are hypotheses. If they cannot be tested at all, they may be dismissed as mere speculation. But if the proposed characteristic can be found in every observed example of existence, then, even though one cannot observe all existence, he can claim that his hypothesis is supported by all the evidence available to him. Since the presence of only one negative instance is sufficient to refute any claim to universality, most proposals will be discarded early. And those that persist by surviving every test to which they are put can, even in the absence of testing them on every existent in the universe, properly be called "knowledge."

Contrary to opinion, metaphysical hypotheses are not the most difficult to test. Instead, they are the most easy. For whereas the hypotheses proposed in the specialized sciences pertain to kinds of existences which are less than all, metaphysical hypotheses about categories of existences pertain to all existences of whatever kind, including those occurring in each person's present experience. That is, if one now experiences anything that exists (and surely he does unless he momentarily experiences a blank), all the categories of existence must be present in it. Of course, if he fails to look for them, he will fail to see them. And if he does not know what to look for, he may not see what is there to determine if he did know. But if, for example, one can give his attention to the temporal character of his experience, he may then observe that whatever exists in it is characterized temporarily also. The point is that, although one may propose hypotheses about categories of existence that are somehow both universally present and yet unobservable, at least all hypotheses about observable categories of existence can be tested by anyone at any time simply by making deliberate observations about what he observes as existing in his present experience. In this sense metaphysical hypotheses are the easiest of all hypotheses to test. Consequently each person can quite easily make considerable headway for himself by eliminating all suggested proposals that do not pass the tests of his own immediate experience of existence.

5 / METAPHYSICS VERSUS ONTOLOGY AND COSMOLOGY

Since the terms "ontology" and "cosmology" are sometimes employed in dealing with metaphysical questions, some explanation of why they are neglected here is called for.

What is meant by *ontology*, the "science of being," depends on what is meant by "being." If "being" and "existence" are synonyms, then "metaphysics" and "ontology" are synonyms; and metaphysics could be defined as "the science of being" just as well as "the science of existence." However, if one considers "being" as that which "has the characteristics," thereby distinguishing between "being" and "its categories," "ontology" and "metaphysics" (inquiry into categories) become distinguishable sciences, each performing a separate function. The reader is warned that he may misunderstand what he reads if he does not keep in mind how different authors use these terms. I prefer the term "existence" partly because for me "existence" includes its categories; so no matter how distinct the words may be, existence is inseparable from its categories and its categories are inseparable from it.

Another reason why I prefer not to use the term "ontology" is that some who emphasize the distinction between "being" and its characteristics do so because they believe that "pure being" or "being itself" can somehow be discovered or at least somehow postulated as a necessary preconception. Since, if I may permit one of my own conclusions to prejudice my definition of metaphysics, I believe that "pure being" or, for that matter, "pure" anything, except as an ideal does not exist, thus, I see no virtue in the quest for it and believe that we are better off if we do not distinguish ontology as a separate science. If nothing can exist without being, then being is a universal characteristic of existence. So, in what follows, I shall regard "being" as a category of existence, and I shall not employ the term "ontology" except when quoting others who do use it.

Cosmology is the "science of the structure of the universe." In early days, when the name "philosopher" applied to a kind of catch-all scientist, speculations about the stars and the physical universe were considered part of his job. Astronomy, now developed as a separate science, has taken over the problems traditionally associated with "cosmology." Whether cosmology is a part of astronomy or vice versa, I leave to the astronomers to settle. But I, at least, do not include cosmological problems under the heading of metaphysics, except in the sense that any conclusions about the nature of existence generally must apply to cosmic existences also; and the metaphysician has not completed his tests about the universality of any proposed category of existence until he has observed its presence among such cosmic existences also.

PART ONE

PROCESS

6 / THINGS

An inquiry into the nature of existence requires a language in which to express its problems as well as its proposed solutions. When we ask, "What exists?" we can obviously answer that "Existences exist." But we prefer the more commonplace language: "Things exist."

By *things* we mean what is completely general or what is meant in common by "thing" as part of the words "something," "anything," "everything," and "nothing." Whatever *is* in any way, whether as a substance or an event, as a dream or an institution, as a person or the universe, is a "thing." Metaphysics, then, is an inquiry into the nature of things, that is, of things and their categories or universal characteristics. We shall ask whether sameness and difference are characteristics of all things, whether change and permanence are characteristics of all things, and whether wholeness and partiality are characteristics of all things.

In our language, then, thingness is itself a category of existence, but we shall speak as if the categories are characteristics of things.

The word "thing" has had a long etymological history, which we shall not trace here. But it may be worth observing how the basic stem, "th," functions as a definite article in English grammar, that is, as "the." Earlier in history we spoke of "thee" and "thou," of "thy" and "thine," and we still speak of "this," "that," "these," "those," "then," "there," and "thus." The Greek word for god is *theos*. And we have adopted as a technical term, both in dialectic and in dissertation writing, "thesis."

We might have chosen the word "being," and said that "Beings exist." Hidden, or forgotten, difficulties with both "thing" and "being" can be revealed by observing that, whereas "th" is regarded as neutral, adding "ing," connoting present continuing verbal tense, the "th" appears to take on the character of a noun, and that the two together, "th" and "ing" as "th-ing," combine both nominal and verbal functions in one word. This works well, except that persistent usage has come to regard the word "thing" as itself a noun, as when we speak of "a thing" or "things," and to describe what a thing does by means of another verb.

The same is true of "be," which I take to be neutral, but which, when we add the verbal ending "ing," in "be-ing," then functions as a noun. Again, common usage treats the word "being" itself as a noun, which we then proceed to describe by a verb; for example, "This being changes." We may observe, also, that "th" is replaced by "de" and its derivatives in Latin and English words inherited therefrom, and that "el" and its variations (al, il, ol, ul) serve the same function in Semitic and Romance languages. Other such general-purpose words can be found. But I propose to use the word "things" as a most general term for our purposes.

7 / DIFFERENCES

With which proposed category shall we begin? If all categories are equally universal, one should be as good as another to start with. My choice is doubly motivated: No other proposed categories are more simple and more obvious to common sense. Descriptions of all other categories involve them.

Surely no words are more useful, not merely in philosophy and in the sciences, but throughout life, than "same" and "different." "Sameness" is something common to all occasions in which two or more things are the same. "Difference" is something common to all occasions in which two or more things are different. By beginning with "sameness" and "difference," the reader should feel at home with such familiar terms.

The Meaning of Sameness and Difference

Let us explore some questions that have been raised about sameness and difference.

1. When we say that two things are the same, do we mean that they are partly the same or completely the same? If they were completely the same, they would be one rather than two. If they are two, they must be at least different enough to be two. Thus the most completely same that two things can be involves some difference.

When we say that two things are different, do we mean that they are partly different or completely different? If they were completely different, they would not be alike in sharing the same relation of difference. Each is like the other at least in being different from the other. The same statement, "Each is different from the other," is true of both of them alike. So the most completely different that two things can be involves some sameness.

Others have expressed these ideas in their own words. Note that the words "sameness," "identity," and "likeness" are used as synonyms; so are "difference," "diversity," and "otherness." "In order to give any real significance to an assertion of identity, it must assert the identity of two diverse things."[1] "Identity is a real union of the diverse."[2] "Otherness . . . is the inseparable spouse of identity: wherever there is identity there is necessarily otherness; and in whatever field there is true otherness there is necessarily identity."[3] "Identity cannot be asserted between two altogether different terms; but it is also meaningless to assert any identity between exactly identical terms; because it would be a needless tautology."[4]

If the reader has encountered usages of the words "sameness," "identity," and "likeness" where they were not regarded as synonyms, he may entertain doubts. If "like" means "partly the same," or if "identical" means "completely the same," then we have further problems. If "like" means "partly the same," then we can restate the question: when we say that two things are alike, do we mean that they are "partly the same in some respect" or "completely the same in that respect"? If we reply "partly the same in some respect," then we seem to be saying that the two things are partly the same in some way in which they are partly the same; whereas if we reply "completely the same in that respect," then at least some "complete sameness" is involved in what we mean by being "alike." If by "identical" we mean "completely the same," we still have two things that are different enough to be two; thus "identity" itself must involve some difference. Nothing is gained in answering our questions by observing that not all persons use these words as synonyms.

2. If, as we have noted, the most completely the same two things can be involves some difference and the most completely different two things can be involves some sameness, do we encoun-

ter any problems by saying that "same means not different" and "different means not same"? Sameness is not difference and difference is not sameness. Sameness and difference are different. Are sameness and difference also the same?

Our first reaction to the question is likely to be no; for any way in which sameness and difference are different, they are obviously not the same. But further exploration may reveal some not-so-obvious samenesses. First, the word "not" has many meanings, whereas we often treat it as if it had only one meaning. Whenever we say that one thing is different from another in any way, we can also say that the one is not the other in that way. If the meaning of "difference" comes in such ways as indicated above, does not the meaning of "not" also come in such ways? If there are degrees of difference, are there not degrees of negation or notness? The prevalence and significance for our purposes of such degrees of notness may be noted in the following.

Consider several pairs of opposites: whole–parts, cause–effect, aim–goal, good–bad, universal–particular. A whole is not its parts and a part is not its whole. A cause is not its effect and an effect is not its cause. An aim is not its goal and a goal is not its aim. Good is not bad and bad is not good. A universal is not one of its particulars and a particular is not its universal. In each of the pairs, one of the two is not the other and so is different from the other; in being different from the other, it is not the same as the other.

Yet is there not something about both of the two in each pair that makes them alike in belonging to that pair? We do not pair "whole" with "effect," "cause" with "goal," "universal" with "bad," even though each is also *not* what we mean by the other. What is meant by "whole" and "parts" and by "cause" and "effect" has a likeness that is missing from "whole" and "effect" and from "parts" and "cause." Fortunately, past usage has provided us with a convenient term to denote this likeness. Although we mean that "whole" and "effect" are opposites in being not each other, what we mean by "whole" and "parts" we call "apposite opposites" to indicate that they also have something in common that makes them more directly opposed to each other than "whole" and "effect." This likeness occurs in what we mean by "sameness" and "difference"; in this way sameness and difference are partly the same.

3. How do sameness and difference exist? When two things are the same in any way, is that sameness a part of each of the two things? Or does that sameness somehow exist apart from each, or both, of the two things? When two things differ in any way, is the way in which they differ a part of each of the two things? Or does it exist somehow apart from each, or both, of them? Although issues raised in later chapters, including those on relations, universals, wholes, time, and dialectic, will have some bearing on how best to answer these questions, one hypothesis presented here is that such sameness and such difference are both parts of the two or more things and also may have a functional nature of their own which, especially when the things and samenesses are more numerous, appears as kinds and serves as bases for laws.

Sameness and Difference as Categories of Existence

Does everything that exists embody some sameness; that is, is it the same as something? Does everything that exists embody some difference; that is, is it such that it is different from something else? If so, then sameness and difference are both universal characteristics of existence, which is what we mean by "category of existence."

We may further ask: Is each thing that exists like every other thing that exists and/or different from every other thing that exists? Is not each thing that exists like every other thing that exists in existing, or in being an existing being; and, if there are categories of existence, is not each existing thing such that it embodies all such categories? Is each thing that exists different from every other thing that exists in being a different thing? No matter how much two things are alike, may they not be sufficiently different to be two? And no matter how much one thing is like all other existing things, must it not be sufficiently different from all of them in order to be itself?

The author proposes the following hypotheses: that both sameness and difference are categories of existence; and that every existing thing is both like every other existing thing in some ways and different from every other existing thing in at least one way. This view appears to have been expressed in the words of others: "Whatever you select...; it will be both identity and difference...."[5] "Existence is always both."[6] "Existence.... Both identity and difference live in its bosom. They are not different from existence as such. They are the form of existence or existence is the form of them."[7] "Existence ... is the union of identity and difference.... It is not properly a blending or mixture of identity and difference; nor on the other hand are identity and difference to be regarded as in reality one.... Its identity is so far from being identical or one with its otherness that it would have no otherness except there were another, and it is other than the other, not the same as the other."[8]

8 / CHANGE

To change is to become different. To become different is to change. To remain the same is to be permanent. To be permanent is to remain the same.

Difference exists. Becoming different exists. Change exists. Sameness exists. Remaining the same exists. Permanence exists.

Without difference, there can be no change. Without sameness, there can be no permanence. But there may be difference without change, because two different things might both be permanent. And there can be sameness with change, for there can be two changes that are alike, or the same, in being changes. Thus there is a sense in which sameness and difference seem more universal than permanence and change. But whenever difference becomes, change occurs; and whenever sameness remains, permanence exists.

Kinds of Change and Permanence

There are as many kinds of change as there are kinds, or ways, of becoming different. The becoming of each difference is a change, and the becomings of each kind of difference constitute a different kind of change.

There are as many kinds of permanence as there are kinds, or ways, of remaining the same. The remaining of each sameness is a permanence, and each kind of remaining the same is a kind of permanence.

Are Change and Permanence Contradictory?

When we say that "a thing changes," does the thing consist entirely in the change, or does the thing continue to exist through the change? If the latter occurs, the thing that changes also remains through the change. It both changes and remains. But change is not permanence and permanence is not change. Can a thing both change and not change at the same time? If we said that "a thing can both change and not change in the same sense at the same time," we would be contradicting ourselves. But when we recognize that the way in which a thing does "not change" when it remains through change and the way in which it does so "change" involve two different senses, we are aware that no contradiction is involved.

Change and Permanence as Categories of Existence

We propose the thesis that "to exist is to change" and, of course, "to change is to exist." It follows from this that there is no existence without change and no nonexisting change. Change and existence involve each other. To change is to become different; so to exist is to become different. Hence existence also involves both difference and becoming, and there are no nonexisting differences or becomings. (Imaginary differences *exist* in the existing imagination.)

We also propose the thesis that "to exist is to be permanent" and that "to be permanent is to exist." It follows from this that there is no existence without permanence and no nonexisting permanence. Permanence and existence involve each other. To be permanent is to remain the same; so to exist is to remain the same; hence existence also involves both sameness and remaining. And there are no nonexisting samenesses or remainings. (If there were nonexisting samenesses, I suppose they could remain nonexisting and could remain the same. But the "were" in this "if" must mean that they exist in some sense, and such speculation seems to involve us in wondering whether there could be some nonexisting existences.)

Having postulated both the thesis that "to exist is to change" and the thesis that "to exist is to be permanent," we have thereby postulated another thesis, namely, that "to exist is both to change and to be permanent" and that "to exist is both to become different and to remain the same." This thesis would be self-contradictory if it asserted that "what exists both changes and is permanent in the same sense at the same time." But "to change" and "to be permanent" are different; so we may say that "what exists may both change and be permanent at the same time" without contradiction, because the sense in which it is permanent and the sense in which it changes are different.

Other Theories of Change and Permanence

The foregoing theses constitute a hypothesis or theory about change that differs from many other theories.

ONLY CHANGE EXISTS; THERE IS NO PERMANENCE. This doctrine is commonly attributed to the early Greek philosopher Heraclitus, who is reported to have said that "All things flow; nothing abides," and that "One cannot step twice in the same river."[1] It is stated explicitly by Theravada Buddhist philosophers as a fundamental principle: "All is impermanent (*anicca*)."[2]

NO CHANGE OCCURS; ALL THAT EXISTS IS PERMANENT. The first Greek proponents of this doctrine were the Eleatics. Parmenides stated that "Being is; nonbeing is not." Being and nonbeing are contradictories. They cannot both be. Therefore, only being is. Change, becoming, or motion are impossible, because they would involve both not being and being which, being contradictories, cannot both be.[3] Zeno defended the doctrine with his famous paradoxes of motion.[4] In India, this view was proclaimed in the Advaita Vedanta of Shankara: "Brahman is eternally accomplished being. It is not becoming."[5] "Change is unreal, since it implies instability, deficiency and incompleteness."[6]

BOTH CHANGE AND PERMANENCE EXIST, BUT NOT IN THE SAME THING. Some things change; others remain permanent; but nothing does both. This theory accepts the view held by the previous two theories, namely, that change and permanence are contradictories; but it rejects their conclusions that since the one exists the other cannot. "One says that all is permanent, another that all is fleeting, and yet another teaches that, of the world and its various elements, some things are fleeting and others ever endure."[7]

CHANGE DEPENDS ON PERMANENCE. "Change by itself, apart from a background of identity, is impossible for the reason that where there is no underlying identity there is nothing to change."[8] "... only what is permanent can change."[9] "The first principle or primary being is not movable either by itself or accidentally.... But since that which is movement must be moved by something, and the first mover must be itself unmovable...."[10] "Movement is dependent upon being because it is always some being that moves or is moved."[11]

PERMANENCE DEPENDS ON CHANGE. "The truth is that we change without ceasing, and that the state itself is nothing but change." "The flux of time is reality itself."[12] "This reality is mobility.... Rest is never more than apparent, or, rather, relative." "With stoppages, however numerous they may be, we shall never make mobility; whereas, if mobility is given, we can, by means of diminution, obtain from it by thought as many stoppages as we desire. In other words, ... concepts may be extracted by our thought from mobile reality; but there are no means of reconstructing with mobility of the real with fixed concepts."[13]

NEITHER CHANGE NOR PERMANENCE EXISTS. This seemingly incomprehensible view is put forth by the Sunyavada or Madhyamika school of Mahayana Buddhism. Reality, *sunya* (void), is devoid of all distinctions. It is pure indistinctness. Because change is not permanence and permanence is not change, each is distinct from the other. All distinction, including the distinction between change and permanence, is illusory. Hence, neither change nor permanence is real. (More fully stated, *sunya* neither is changing, nor is permanent, nor is both changing and permanent, nor is neither changing nor permanent. Although it is included here as a theory, Sunyavadins would prefer to have their view regarded as nontheoretical.)

Both Change and Permanence Exist.   Many authors accept the coexistence of both change and permanence, even if in different ways. "There is no existence that does not possess alike changes and tendencies to maintain unchangeability during the process of change...."[14] "In the phenomenal universe the permanent and the impermanent are indissolubly conjoined."[15] "Permanence and change refer to different aspects...."[16]

Probably most theories do not conform strictly to any of the foregoing types. Some believe that there is more permanence than change, or more change than permanence. Some may hold that at times existence involves more permanence than change and at other times more change than permanence, following the analogy of geological stability interrupted by cataclysmic upheaval or of a long-established society shaken by turbulent revolution. Some see change and permanence always equally present since, dialectically, permanence can continue to exist only through changing times and change can exist only by continuing (that is, remaining, hence being permanent) through time.

9 / SUBSTANCE

The term "substance" has been used in many ways and has been defined relative to other categories also in many ways. We here explore three of these ways and show how they may be expressed in other words as well.

Substance and Other Categories

The three ways of relating pertain to (1) permanence and change, (2) function, and (3) aspects or properties.

RELATIVE TO PERMANENCE AND CHANGE.   To change is to become different and to remain the same is to be permanent. To the extent that anything remains the same, or is permanent, it functions as substantial. To the extent that anything functions as substantial, we may speak of it as a substance.

Since there are as many kinds of permanence as there are kinds of remaining the same, a thing may be substantial in one way and change, or be unsubstantial, in other ways. Being substantial, that is, remaining the same, is being temporal. When some things endure longer than others, they are thereby more substantial because they remain through more temporal changes. There may be momentary substances: If something endures throughout a moment, it is substantial during that moment. And if at the end of the moment there is no *it* that endures, then there is no such substance. Thus some substances are temporary as well as temporal.

RELATIVE TO FUNCTION.   Substance and function are correlative notions. To function is to be or to act (including being aspectival and being acted upon) in any way. Whenever there is functioning, there is that which functions, and that which functions is a substance. A substance is that which functions, and a function is whatever a substance does (in any sense or in any tense of any verb). When anything ceases to function, then it ceases to be substantial or ceases to be a substance and indeed ceases to be. Nothing can be without being substantial in the sense that it functions as remaining as long as it endures, no matter how briefly. In these senses, substance and function are the same as being and doing.

Some persons regard substance and function as such that function depends on substance whereas substance does not depend on function; others regard function as more dependent on substance than substance is on function. However, the view presented here is that substance and function interdepend—there are no completely nonfunctioning substances; there are no completely insubstantial functionings. If to become different is to change and to change is to be insubstantial, we may ask, "Are there insubstantial functionings?" There can be insubstantial functionings only if there are also substantial functionings, that is, substances that remain through change.

Then we can say that "a thing changes," and hence that "a substance changes," only if we recognize that the thing also remains through such change and thus functions substantially through such change in order to function as that which changes or as that which is insubstantial in whatever way it changes. A thing can be both substantial and insubstantial, because it can both remain the same in one way and change in another way. Hence, that which is substantial (that is, the thing), can also be insubstantial in whatever way a change is a change in it. A confused person, for example, may change his mind about an issue several times and may be said to be inconsistent and unsubstantial in his views; but he can do this only by remaining the same person and remaining substantial as a person.

Whenever a new functioning emerges, that which newly functions (a new substance) emerges. Although, as we propose, nothing absolutely new can emerge, whenever a new functioning emerges, the emerging of such novel functioning as part of a preexisting substance (i.e., a thing functioning substantially) involves novel substantiality which may be an additional way in which the thing functions substantially. Hence the new substance may be merely a new (changed) way in which the thing functioning as a substance functions as a substance. Furthermore, if any new substance emerges, it must then newly function as such. Substances and functions emerge together and cease together.

RELATIVE TO ASPECTS. Some persons regard substance and aspects (often called "properties," "qualities," or "attributes") as such that aspects of substances depend on their substances but such that substances do not depend upon their aspects. Others regard aspects as more dependent upon their substances than their substances depend upon their aspects. The view presented here is that substance and aspect interdepend. A thing is substantial by virtue of its continuing to have an aspect. A thing, or substance, consists partly in its aspects and partly in its functioning as that which has such aspects. To be a thing, or substance, is to be aspectival in the sense of being or having aspects.

But, further, insofar as any aspect itself remains through change, it too is substantial. Hence a thing, or substance, can remain substantial in some ways only by having or being substantial aspects. On the other hand, a thing that functions in many ways has each of those ways as aspects or properties of itself. Thus substantiality may be regarded as an aspect or property of a thing and its correlative functionality as another aspect (or property).

A thing is also spatial, relational, causal, particular, and so on. Each of these ways of functioning is aspectival or is an aspect of the thing. Relative to these ways of functioning, being substantial is another aspect of the thing. But each of these ways of functioning is also substantial in whatever way the functioning continues.

That is, a thing is substantially spatial; and its spatial aspects, as continuing, are also substantial. A thing is relational, that is, substantially relational in whatever way its relations continue or remain the same; and its relations are also substantial in whatever way they continue or remain the same. The same may be said of all categories.

Interpreting aspects as "properties" (something owned), a thing belongs to, or is owned by, or is a property of, its aspects as much as its aspects belong to, or are owned by, or are properties of, it. A thing as a substance owns its aspects as properties. But the aspects of a thing as a substance own it as their thing or their substance as well as being owned by it. Thus a thing functions both as a substance owning all of its aspects, including substantiality, as properties and as a property, and thus as an aspect, owned by all of these aspects functioning as substantial, each in its own way as well as jointly.

The mutual ownership of all these aspects by each other constitutes "organicity," which is itself an aspect of that which is substantial, of that which is functional, of that which is spatial, and of that which is thingal. But organicity itself is mutually involved and thus is substantial, functional, spatial, relational, and causal. Organicity, as mutuality of interdependence of each and all of these aspects, is itself owned by them as well as owner of them. It is aspectival to them just as they are aspectival to it. Organicity is substantial to the extent that it involves and is involved in remaining the same through change; a substance is organic to the extent that it involves and is involved in functioning as aspectival to all other aspects that also function substantially, that is, both as aspects per se and as aspects of that of which they are aspects.

Things as substances may have negative aspects, such as the absence of some part or aspect. For example, a person with a permanently missing tooth is substantially toothless relative to that tooth. A vacancy, absence, or cessation may be substantial. Death is substantial.

Other Theories of Substance

Aristotle says that "it is a distinctive mark of substance that, while remaining numerically one and the same, it is capable of admitting contrary qualities, the modification taking place through a change in the substance itself."[1] Such a statement, including "remaining the same . . . through a change" and having different "qualities," is similar to the foregoing view (relative to permanence and change and to aspects or qualities). Aristotle, however, adds conditions which the foregoing view finds unacceptable: (1) "Substance does not admit of variation of degree."[2] My view is that a thing that is substantial may become more substantial or less substantial in various ways, including ceasing to be substance. (2) Some substances are "primary," (are "entities which underlie everything else . . ."), and others are "secondary." My view is that, although some substances (for example, categories of existence) last longer than others, each substance, or each thing that is substantial, is primary in its own way. (3) "Another mark of substance is that it has no contrary."[3] In other words, there is no such thing as insubstantiality. My view is that things may be substantial and insubstantial in various ways, both at the same time.

Aristotle further states that "all substance appears to signify that which is individual."[4] I do not object to this, for each thing or substance is an individual or particular thing or substance. But if this statement is intended to rule out universals,[5] then I do object. For if the sameness which two or more things have in common constitutes a universal, then such universality has as much substantiality as do those two or more things while they remain the same.

Several other theories about the nature of substance have developed from emphasizing one or another of the aspects involved in Aristotle's complicated treatment of the subject.

THAT IN WHICH QUALITIES (PROPERTIES) INHERE.   John Locke

referred to substance as an "unknown support" in which qualities inhere. Substance in this sense is needed to hold the qualities or properties together and to stand under or support them while they exist.[6]

"THE UNDERLYING REALITY" ON WHICH ALL THINGS DEPEND. Aristotle called this "primary substance." Theories differ regarding the nature of this "reality," or "stuff of which everything is made," and whether only one, two, or many such ultimate substances exist.

THAT WHICH "STANDS BY ITSELF."   Derived doubtless from the view that qualities depend on substance for support but that substance does not depend on qualities for support, this view holds that substance is that which does not depend and hence "stands by itself."[7] Spinoza carried out the logical implications of this theory, concluding that there can be only one substance, the universe, which he called "Nature" or "God."[8]

These theories in my view exemplify reductionistic oversimplifications. Things are substantially multifunctional; and all the categories of existence are substantial aspects of things but in another sense are substances themselves. A thing or substance cannot be fully understood until its interdependence with all other categories of existence is also understood.

10 / WHOLES

No problem is more central to understanding the nature of existence, or knowledge, or values, or logic than the problem of the nature and relations of a whole and its parts, and of wholeness and partiality.

Interrelations of Wholes and Parts

On the one hand, it is clear immediately that by a *part* we mean that it is "a part of a whole," and that by a *whole* we mean that it is "a whole of parts." Given these meanings, there are no parts that are not parts of a whole and no wholes that are not wholes of parts. Whole and parts involve each other; each depends on the other for being, even though each is not the other. A part of a whole is not that whole, and a whole of parts is not one of its parts.

Difficulties in conceiving just how a whole and its parts are related to each other, however, have given rise to theories which seem to deny, or at least modify, what is initially obvious. Some of the difficulties arise because there are different kinds of wholes and whole–part relations.

We consider three kinds here: "the aggregate, the mechanical whole, and the organic whole. In an aggregate the parts are absolutely independent of each other, both functionally and existentially."[1] Whether or not an aggregate or collection can exist in such a way that "the parts are absolutely independent of each other," we do often think of parts of collections, such as marbles in a box or cars in a parking lot, as completely independent of each other. In elementary mathematics, one learns about numbers that "the whole is equal to the sum of its parts."[2] We shall use the word "whole" to mean "all of the parts." Now one may raise the question of whether every all is a whole. It may be that every all which is thought is in some sense a whole without any existing wholeness in any collection of things. Yet, on the other hand, if the collection is one in which all members have one or more characteristics in common, such characteristic(s) may serve to unify them in a way that constitutes a kind of wholeness. In any case, a collection or aggregate of things is not very much of a whole of parts when compared with wholes of other kinds.

"In a mechanical whole, such as a watch, the parts depend on each other, functionally, but are independent existentially."[3] In a mechanism such as an automobile one part, such as a wheel, piston, or steering rod, may be taken out and replaced by a like part without changing the nature of either the whole or any of the parts. Automobiles speeding on a freeway operate as functional wholes. Each is a whole with its own parts. Each would cease to function as a whole if any one of its essential parts ceased to remain a part of it. An automobile repair shop has its parts department. And a person may replace many of the parts of his car. One mechanic is said to have replaced the parts of his car, one or a few at a time, until he had replaced every one of them. Presumably he still had "the same car," that is, the same whole with completely different parts. When he became unemployed, he gathered up all of the replaced parts and reassembled them, and then he had two cars. Functionally he had an entirely new car, but all the parts had been parts of his first car. Exchange of like parts does not change the nature of a mechanical whole.

"In an organic whole, the mutual dependence of the parts and the whole is complete.... The organic whole is completely dependent on its parts, just as much as the parts are dependent on the whole."[4] When a whole and its parts are completely dependent on each other, a change in one, either a part or the whole, involves a change in the other. When an organic whole, such as a biological organism, loses a part such as an arm, an eye, or a lung, it becomes a partly different whole. Its becoming a partly different whole in turn has effects on its other parts; the other arm, eye, or lung, for example, is required to do extra work. When we understand organic wholes, we recognize that we are involved with two kinds of wholes, namely, the whole that is the whole of parts and the whole (i.e., the organic whole) that is the whole inclusive of the whole of parts and the parts. In order to avoid confusion, it is better to speak of the latter whole as an "organism." (Note that here we use "organism" as a general metaphysical term for all organic wholes, that is, all wholes that include both a whole and its parts, rather than as it is sometimes used to include merely biological organisms.)

An organism consists both of a whole and its parts or, if you prefer, both of the parts of a whole and the whole of those parts and of course their interdependent relations. The differences between the parts remain as constituents of the organic whole; and the difference between the whole and its parts remains as a constituent of the organic whole. An organism is an organization of parts of a whole in which the parts remain parts and do not become the whole, and of a whole and its parts in which the whole remains a whole and does not become one of its parts. Yet in the organism both the whole and its parts function as parts of it as an organic whole. In an organism, the whole is different from its parts and the parts are different from the whole. But an organism includes both the whole and its parts and their differences from each other. A part and a whole are polarly related, but an organic whole includes that polarity and all the other polar relations of each part to the whole. Hence the concept of an organism, or organic whole, even apart from other categories, is very complex. It is understandable that people look for simpler conceptions in attempting to understand the nature of things.

Other Theories of Wholes and Parts

Let us explore some theories of the nature of wholes and parts. First, we will observe attempts to escape the difficulties involved in relating whole and parts by going to the extremes of denying existence to either the whole or the parts.

ONLY PARTS EXIST; NO WHOLES EXIST. The early Greek philosophers Leucippus and Democritus explained existence as consisting of innumerable hard particles, which they called "atoms," meaning uncuttables or indivisibles. In this view, stones, animals, and ideas are all somehow accidental temporary aggregates of these particles and have no wholeness. Curiously, those who believe that there can be parts without wholes seem to be involved in holding that each such part is itself a whole, that is, an indivisible whole, which is thus a whole without parts.

ONLY THE WHOLE EXISTS; NO PARTS EXIST. I know of no one who holds this view as stated. Yet tendencies toward such a view appear in some followers of Advaita Vedanta when they describe ultimate reality (*Nirguna Brahman*) as pure indistinctness. *Nirguna Brahman* has no parts. But, as we shall see below, the Advaitins have a more subtle view than this. Each liberated soul (*purusha*) is partless for the Sanhya-Yoga school. Plotinus' ultimate reality, "The One," is partless. "We are necessarily led to call this 'The One' in our discussions the better to designate 'partlessness' while we strive to bring our minds to 'oneness.' "[5] Thomas Aquinas held that the soul is simple; hence it is without parts.

WHOLES DEPEND ON PARTS MORE THAN PARTS DEPEND ON WHOLES. The Emergentists, including S. Alexander, C. Lloyd Morgan, and R. W. Sellars, depict emergence of new levels of being, or beings at new levels (e.g., life emerging from the physical level or mind emerging from the biological level) as involving new organizations of parts. An animal functions as an individual, a whole being, but his wholeness depends on the parts, the organs, cells, molecules, atoms, and electrons. Some, if not all, of the electrons, atoms, and molecules that comprise the body could exist even if the animal did not exist; but the animal could not exist if the necessary electrons, atoms, and molecules did not exist as its parts. The higher the level of emergence, proceeding from physical to biological to psychological to social, the more complicated the organization and thus the more intricate the whole. But no whole fails to continue to be completely dependent on its parts, whereas some of its parts, at least, can continue to exist even without the whole.

PARTS DEPEND ON WHOLES MORE THAN WHOLES DEPEND ON PARTS. "We have next to consider the important principle that the Whole alone can be fully real. It follows that we can only understand the true nature of any particular manifestation in the universe if we know the character of that universe as a whole."[6] "The whole is what yields the parts, not the parts the whole."[7] "The fundamental 'formula' of Gestalt theory might be expressed in this way: There are wholes, the behavior of which is not determined by that of their individual elements, but where the part-processes are themselves determined by the intrinsic nature of the whole."[8]

PARTS AND WHOLES BOTH EXIST, BUT THEY HAVE NOTHING IN COMMON. "The antinomy between whole and parts . . . had its roots in the conception of whole and parts as inevitably exclusive of one another, the whole being regarded as prior to the parts or the parts as prior to the whole."[9] Few, if any, hold this extreme view; but when the difference between a whole and its parts, each of which is not the other, is stressed, one may think of this difference as exclusive.

NEITHER PARTS NOR WHOLES EXIST. Advaita Vedanta holds that the ultimate reality, *Nirguna Brahman*, involves no distinctions and thus no distinction between whole and parts. "It cannot be regarded as a whole including parts . . . ,"[10] for "it transcends the opposition of ... whole and part...."[11] " 'Part' and 'whole' are not true or real entities, but only 'things of reason,' and consequently there are in Nature neither whole nor parts."[12] Madhyamika Buddhists regard ultimate reality (*sunya*) as void of distinctions and hence indescribable. If we insist on attempting to describe it, we may say that it is, or has, neither parts, nor a whole, nor both parts and a whole, nor neither parts nor a whole.

BOTH PARTS AND WHOLE EXIST INTERDEPENDENTLY. Each depends on the other. Yet, each is also different from the other and is in some sense independent of the other. For interdependence involves both partial independence and partial dependence. Each whole, although different from its parts, is what it is as a whole of parts because of the parts and the nature of the parts of which it is a whole. And each part, although different from the whole and from every other part, is what it is as a part of that whole of parts partially as a result of the nature of the other parts and of the whole. "The very meaning of a part implies that it must be determined or conditioned by other parts."[13]

Of course, various kinds of wholes, parts, and whole–part relations exist. Some parts are much more dependent on their wholes than other parts (e.g., an infant usually is more dependent on its family than a 20-year-old child). Some wholes are more dependent on some parts than upon other parts (e.g., a body usually is more dependent upon its heart than on one of its hands).

Wholes, Parts, and Other Categories

Does change in a part cause a change in the whole? Does a change in the whole cause a change in the parts (some or all)? Which is more permanent, the whole or its parts (some or all)? Which has more power to influence the other causally, a whole or its parts?

Are a whole and its parts equally temporal? That is, do they share the same present, or does each part and the whole have its own kinds of change and time? Does not the whole of a person's lifetime last longer than the birth and death of one of his cells or than the supposed spin of one of his subatomic particles? On the other hand, may not some stable molecules exist prior to a person's birth, enter his body for a while, and continue to exist after his death?

Are parts and whole spatially related? Are the parts contained spatially within the whole? Does the space constituting the whole exist prior to the spatial relations between the parts or does it result from their constituting the whole? Do spatial relations internal to a part, insofar as it is partly independent of the whole, also participate as part of the space constituting the space internal to the whole?

These questions receive somewhat different answers by the above alternative theories of the nature of wholes and parts. Hence, it is necessary to explore all the other categories before it is possible fully to comprehend the nature of wholes and parts. Especially significant are questions about levels, involving wholes within wholes within wholes, and so on, and parts of wholes, which are parts of wholes, which are parts of wholes, and so on. Is each part of a whole also a whole? Can there be a smallest part that is, in a sense, a whole without parts? Is there a largest whole? Involved here are questions of how variations in influences of different parts of one whole on each other affect not only that whole but also the whole of which it is a part and other higher-level wholes. If a whole and its parts interdepend, and if such a whole is also an interdependent part of a larger whole, and so on, then its parts interdepend also with the whole of which it is a part, and so on. The intricacies of such interdependencies are only beginning to be explored.

II / TIME

The problem of time is difficult to deal with, partly because it is really several problems. Some that will be considered here include: events and duration; how long is the present? simultaneity; levels of time; does the past exist? can there be eternity without time? instantaneity. The hypotheses proposed will be followed by a summary of other theories of time.

Events and Duration

EVENTS. "Every change is an event."[1] And every event is a change. There are as many events as there are changes and as many changes as there are events. Since (as stated previously) to change is to become different and to become different is to change, there are as many events as there are ways of becoming different and as many ways of becoming different as there are events.

DURATION. To endure, or to have or be duration, is to remain the same; and to remain the same is to endure, or to be or have duration. Each remaining-the-same in any respect is an endurance or a duration, and each duration is a remaining-the-same. Since (as stated previously) to remain the same is to be permanent and to be permanent is to remain the same, then to endure or to be a duration is to be permanent and to be permanent is to endure or to be a duration. So there are as many durations as there are permanences or ways of remaining the same, and there are as many permanences or ways of remaining the same as there are durations.

44

Some events take longer than others to occur. Some durations last longer than others. Postponing exploration of how "take longer" and "last longer" exist, we may here observe that an event takes longer to occur when and because a difference takes longer to become and that a duration lasts longer when and because a sameness lasts longer (i.e., remains the same longer).

INTERDEPENDENCE. Events and durations do not exist in isolation from each other; they interdepend. Not only does an event consist in the becoming of a difference, but also (unless such a becoming were merely instantaneous, i.e., took no time at all to become) such an event remains the same event from the beginning of its becoming to the end of its becoming. Since every remaining-the-same constitutes a duration, each event involves whatever duration exists from its beginning to its end. In this way every event involves duration. No events exist without duration, because (if I may here insert another hypothesis concerning existence) there are no merely instantaneous events. Not only does each duration consist in a remaining-the-same, but also (unless such a remaining had no beginning or end, i.e., has remained the same forever and will remain the same forever) each duration has a beginning and an end. Hence each duration involves at least two events—the event of the becoming of the difference consisting of its first not being a duration and then being a duration (from "is not" a duration to "is" a duration), and the event of the becoming of the difference consisting of its being a duration and then not being a duration (from "is" a duration to "is not" a duration). In this way every duration involves events. No duration exists without events, because (if I may here introduce another hypothesis about existence) no duration exists entirely without any beginning and entirely without any ending.

ASPECTS. Events and durations are aspectival, not merely in the sense of being aspects of each other but in the sense that both are aspects of something that exists and therefore embodies also all the other categories of existence as aspects. That is, time, whatever its nature, includes not merely the interdependence of events and duration but also the dependence of these on, or rather the interdependence of these with, all other categories of existence. No attempt to interpret the nature of time apart from the remainder of existence can ever be adequate. Part of the reason that so many theories fail to be satisfactory is that they assume some part of the nature of time to be fundamental and then attempt to explain other parts as dependent on it and other categories as dependent on it, omitting recognition of several varieties of interdependence.

Part of the problem of interpreting the nature of time, or of any category, consists of referring to it as "it" (i.e., as "something") when such reference takes the grammatical form of a noun, which in Indo-European languages tends to connote substantiality. The hypothesis proposed here needs a language structured in a way that reflects the structure of existence it proposes rather than a "subject–predicate" language based on a "substance–attribute" metaphysics, which it is criticizing. An Esperanto-type language, in which all stems may function as nouns, verbs, adjectives, and adverbs, is needed, but some way of connoting conjoint functioning of all ways at the same time is also needed. Development of the implicit aspect-logic must await another work, although some understanding of its nature will be presupposed in exploring metaphysical categories here; as an abstracted generalization about the structure of existence as experienced, it will presuppose the metaphysical hypotheses proposed here.

EVENTITY.   Although no general name, except perhaps "existence" itself, is likely to be satisfactory to connote all categories of existence as aspects of existence and as aspectivally interdependent, we may try to find a name to express the persisting mutual interdependence of apposite opposites constituting a dimension. Events and duration, according to the present hypotheses, are apposite opposites. Each is not the other; hence they are opposites. But they are alike in sharing the constituting of time; hence they function appositely. Some conjunctive term such as "evenduration" or "duravent" is needed; but since earlier I have adopted another term, "eventity," conjoining the meanings of "event" and "entity," convenience motivates reference to it here.[2]

Entity connotes being, or enduring being, and thus substance, and we can observe that substance, as something that remains through change, presupposes permanence and duration. Thus the conjoint term "eventity" connotes both events and duration as polar opposites functioning as interdependent aspects of something that both have, or are, in common. Hence when we speak of "each eventity," we shall be connoting the interdependence of both the eventive and durational aspects of time.

Another problem in referring to time becomes troublesome when we cite examples (one of the reasons for omitting examples thus far). On investigation, each example of "an event" is likely to be found to be a whole galaxy of events. So for purposes of abstract understanding, we must extract the barest essentials for analytic examination. Let us take as a familiar example of "an event" a blink of an eyelid. If to change is to become different and if every change is an event, then every becoming different, from *is not* to *is* or from *is* to *is not*, is an event. A blink involves at least two events; first the eyelid is opened and then closed and, second, the eyelid is closed and then opened; and at least two durations, the duration of the closing of the eyelid and the duration of the opening of the eyelid (and any duration involved in any pause between opening and closing). Yet a blink occurs so rapidly, relative to other observed events, that we normally automatically interpret it as a single event. In whatever sense it is "an" event, that is, has a singleness, unity, or wholeness about it, it also has a singleness, unity, or wholeness of its duration. That is, as "an" event, it remains the same from beginning to end.

Thus each example of "an event" is likely to be found to be a galaxy of eventities, that is, of many interdependent events and durations, some succeeding and some overlapping or even encompassing others. How this happens shall become clearer when we discuss "levels of time." How such a complex eventity can also properly be called "an" event may become clearer by reviewing our treatment of the "whole–part" polarity.[3]

How Long Is the Present?

An event endures long enough to happen; thereby it begins to occur, endures, and ends its endurance and occurrence. It is present in existence, or has present existence, from its beginning (but not before its beginning) until its ending (but not after its ending). Each event is present in existence as long as it actually exists. Since some changes take longer to occur, and some events last longer than others, some events are present in existence longer than others. The present of an event that lasts longer than another is a longer present than the present of the other. Each event is, or has, its own present. There is no absolutely universal present, of either limited or infinitesimal duration, that restricts the length of all events.

We can easily observe some events, such as a blink, the pulse of a heartbeat, or even an inhalation; they occur within a present experience, and we may be able to observe two or more such events within one present experience. But other events, such as getting out of bed in the morning, tend to require a series of acts of attention and some memory and conceptualization in order to be observed. Still others, such as a day (e.g., a day–night cycle), a lunar month, a crop season, or a solar year, involve more complicated generalizations. A present year is the same year all year, just as the present day is the same day all day, and a present heartbeat is the same heartbeat from its beginning to its end. So we have a present heartbeat, a present day, and a present year. Either there is no "the present," or each present is its own "the present." We properly speak of a "present civilization," a "present life," as well as of a "present day" or a "present moment." Each is an event; each endures; each is an eventity.

Simultaneity

Two or more things are simultaneous when they occur at the same time. Since each of two events has its own time, or its own present, any statement about two events being simultaneous presupposes some basis for comparison of times or presents. We may compare one of two events with the other, in which case the other is taken as the basis for comparison; we may now say that the one is or is not simultaneous with the other. Or we may compare the other with the one, in which case the one is taken as the basis for comparison; we may now say that the other is or is not simultaneous with the one.

When two persons are attending to their breathing and controlling their inhalation–exhalation rates, one may observe that his breath cycle is longer than, or shorter than, or of the same length as that of the other. They may, accidentally or deliberately, have breath cycles that begin at the same time and end at the same time and thus last for the same length of time. The two such breath cycles are observed to be simultaneous. We may say that one exists at the same time as the other, or that the other exists at the same time as the one, or that both exist at the same time, in which case we can generalize that if the one is the same as the other and the other is the same as the one, there is some single sameness (or same sameness) involved in two such samenesses.

When one event, such as inhalation by one person, is observed both to begin before and to end after an otherwise simultaneous event, such as inhalation by another person, the latter is observed to exist for a shorter time when compared with the former and the former to exist for a longer time when compared with the latter. We here observe that, although the shorter event exists at the same time as the longer event while the shorter event exists (and in this sense may be said to be simultaneous with it), the longer event exists also before and after the shorter event and thus exists at a time that is not the same as, or is not simultaneous with, the shorter event. Hence the longer event is both simultaneous with the shorter event while the shorter event lasts and is not simultaneous with it when the longer event exists before and after it.

When one event, such as inhalation by one person, is observed to endure while several events, such as several inhalations by other panting persons occur, the former is simultaneous with, for example, three of the latter in the sense that it continues to exist during the existence of each of them even though they succeed each other in such a way that one of them ceases to exist before the other begins and in such a way that they are not simultaneous with each other. And each of the three is in one sense simultaneous with the one longer event, which is both simultaneous with each of them in succession while each exists and also not simultaneous with each of them in whatever way it exists before and after each of them.

Levels of Time

In addition to observations about simultaneous events, such as inhalations or heartbeats of two persons, we may observe that more complex events occur in such a way as to include and to be constituted by relatively simpler and shorter events, such as the several spasms constituting an orgasm. The latter may be spoken of as having a higher level of time in the sense that it is constituted by all the others each occurring for a shorter time. Or, comparing all the heartbeats as events within a lifetime, which may also be regarded as an event, the latter is a higher, or more inclusive, level of time.

Each complex eventity that depends for its existence on all of several constituent eventities is a temporally higher-level eventity in this sense. The life of a person's body depends on the occurrence of the events within each of its cells, which in turn depend on the occurrence of events within each of the molecules constituting the cells, which in turn depend on the occurrence of

events within the atoms constituting the molecules, which ulti-
mately depend on the subatomic particles constituting such atoms,
if our usual picture of biological, chemical, and physical structures
is correct. Likewise, our galaxy presumably is an eventity constituted by stellar systems such as our solar system, which is constituted by sun and planets including our earth, which are constituted by molecules, atoms, particles, and so on. As persons, we
exist, apparently, within one or more hierarchical systems of levels
of time, such that events in particles, atoms, and cells are events
within the event of our lifetime, while our lives are events occurring within geological, solar, and galactic events.

Thus there is a sense in which an event in a subatomic particle
constituent of a body is simultaneous with a life, even if with only
a tiny portion of it, and a sense in which that life is simultaneous
with the event now enduring as our galaxy, even with only a tiny
portion of it. But when so many subatomic events come and go
during one lifetime, and when life is so short compared with the
duration of our galaxy, the nonsimultaneous aspects of my life
when compared with subatomic and galactic events are more numerous. Although relatively isolated or unrelated temporal systems
also exist, such as my life and the life of an Eskimo who lived
all his life near the Arctic Circle and died on the day I was born, I
believe that the nature of time can be understood better by observing the interrelations of higher and lower levels of time in
which we participate more obviously.

Does the Past Exist?

By "past" we mean "not present" in the sense of no longer
present. For example, we distinguish between present and past
events (such as heartbeats or inhalations) today, between today
and past days in the present month, between the present month
and past months in the present year, and between the present
year and past years in a present lifetime. What is regarded as past

relative to one of the aforementioned distinctions appears to be regarded as also present, or simultaneous, relative to the later distinctions.

For example, the expired days of the present lunar month are past when compared with today but are simultaneous with the month in the sense that all of them occurred within the same month which, as an event, is a unity. But they are also not simultaneous with the month in the sense that they also do not exist during the other days when each of them, in turn, is simultaneous with the month. That which is past relative to one eventity (e.g., a day) may also exist as simultaneous with that which is present in another eventity, such as a month, in whatever sense the other eventity is a unit. If the other eventity is a unit that cannot be broken into parts and still exist as such a unit, then it is the same unit from beginning to end and as such is a temporal unity properly described as present. All lesser eventities that occur serially as constituents of it (e.g., as days in a month) are simultaneous with it as a unit of time, while being successive to each other in terms of their own units of time. In fact, a month appears to require the existence simultaneous with it of the multiplicity of 28 consecutive days in order for it to exist as a month.

Just as each eventity has its own present, so each has its own past; or "the past" is always something relative to a present. Usually the term "the past" connotes "all that is past." That is, relative to today, "the past" includes not only "the past day" but "all past days"; and relative to the present year, "the past" includes not only "the past year" but "all past years." Just as we generalize about what is common to several presents (such as present inhalations, present days, present months, and present years) and speak ambiguously of "the present" relative to which particular present we have in mind, so we generalize about what is common to several pasts (such as past inhalations, past days, past months, and past years) and speak ambiguously of "the past" relative to which particular past we have in mind.

There exists no absolutely universal past such that, when one eventity ceases to exist and becomes past, all other eventities that were in any sense simultaneous with it must also immediately cease to exist and become totally past. However, there is a sense in which "the past" is absolute, namely, that when an eventity has occurred and ceased to exist, it will never recur or exist again as a present eventity.

. If we wish to speculate about existence as a whole, we can deduce implications of our theory relative to it. If existence as a whole is such that some of its aspects, i.e., those which are cate-goreal, never change, then their continuing existence constitutes an everlasting present which, as aspectival to existence that also always was and will be changing, can be regarded as eventitive. If, on the other hand, existence as a whole is such that sooner or later all its aspects change, so that there are no categoreal aspects of existence as a whole, then when any one kind of aspect ceases to exist entirely, an absolutely universal past exists relative to that kind of aspect in the sense that no aspect of such kind will ever exist again.

When two eventities terminate at the same time relative to each other, they become past simultaneously. When one terminates before the other, it becomes past before the other becomes past; and the other remains in existence after the first has become past. Hence some of what is past is contemporaneous with some of what is present; and some of what is present is contemporaneous with some of what is past. Surely at least that part of what is past which is contemporaneous with what is present does exist, even if it "exists as past." Whereas today exists as present both as a day in itself and as a day in the present month, yesterday does not exist as present as a day in itself but does exist as absent and, as past, as a day in the present month.

Continuing our speculations about existence as a whole, we can infer as follows: If the same principle holds relative to past months in the present year, past years in the present century, past centuries in the present millennium, and so on, if there is some longest, everlasting eventity within which all other eventities occur, then they all can exist as past in the sense that they continue to be simultaneous with it as an existing unit. If, on the other hand, there is no temporal unity of existence as a whole, and if some eventities become past for so long that they are not contemporaneous with anything that exists, then, in this sense, such eventities do not exist even as past. This latter view involves certain epistemological difficulties, for if I say that Brutus killed Caesar on the Ides of March in a certain century and my statement is true, something must exist in some sense or other to make the statement true. Either what is past *must* exist in some sense, or there can be no true statements about the past. Either the past exists in some sense, or there is no past. To say that there is a past that does not in any sense exist appears to be a self-contradictory statement.

The past grows, and it keeps growing. At least it grows in the sense that more of what is now present ceases to be present and becomes past. The past becomes longer as more present eventities cease and become added to it. The past seems to be endless in one sense, namely, that what is present unendingly becomes past. Eventities that became past long ago, such as the death of Abraham Lincoln, keep changing in the sense that, with the passage of each present day, the day of his death becomes one day farther from the present day. Not only do persons who remain alive become a day older each day, but also persons who are dead become a day older as dead each day. Thus the past is dynamic as well as static. Eventities that are past never cease to be past and so are static in this sense. The view proposed here involves a double-aspect theory of the past as well as of the present.

Can There Be Eternity without Time?

The view proposed here rejects the notion of an eternity as a single timeless being existing apart from time. To exist is to be temporal. Yet time has two aspects: duration and change. If by "eternal" we mean "duration without change" (which appears to be what is meant by "eternal" even by those who posit the existence of a single timeless being), then are there not as many eternities as there are durations without change? If each eventity involves two aspects, one of which is enduring in some sense without change from beginning to end, does not each eventity thereby involve being eternal in that sense? Hence by partially redefining "the eternal" and by relocating it as an aspect of each eventity, this view not only sees a multiplicity of eternities, one as an aspect of each eventity, but also must assert that there is nothing that is not in this sense eternal.

This theory claims that traditional views reflect what A. N. Whitehead calls the "fallacy of simple location" regarding eternity. That is, they locate the eternal outside of time and hence equate it with timelessness, rather than observe it as an aspect of each eventity, as proposed here. Some events take longer to happen than others. Hence some eternities are durations without change that last longer than others in the sense that they remain unchanged while many more changes ocur. Eternities are quanta, not quantities, of time. Events, that is, the changing aspects of eventities, are quantitative in the sense that they come and go, succeeding each other, by the becoming of differences. Time involves both a quantitative, or changing, aspect and a quanta-tive, or unchanging aspect. As quantitative, time is measurable. As quanta-tive, time is immeasurable, for quanta are undivided.

Heartbeats, days, years, and lifetimes, though each remains in some sense unchanged long enough for it to happen, come and go millions of times while the earth continues to exist in some sense unchanged from its beginning to its end. The earth in contrast is everlasting in the sense that it remains while all of these come and go. Its endurance without change is an eternity; and relative to the lives that are born and die, its eternity seems monolithic and enduring before and after, and thus in a sense outside of, their times. Yet, presumably the earth too is an eventity that once did not exist and that again will not exist. That there are more enduring eventities, such as galaxies, our astronomers now do not doubt.

Whether there are some categories of existence that never have changed and never will change, we can only speculate. If so, then they are eternal, most eternal. If not, then, to put the matter paradoxically, change is a more enduring aspect of existence than duration without change. But is not the enduringness of change, not of a particular change but of changingness as a category of existence, itself an example of an unchanging category? Must there not be, then, some aspectival longest duration without change, or something that, though never separate from other aspects of time, remains permanently unchanging or eternal?

Instantaneity

An instant, sometimes considered an infinitesimal amount of time or as a point in duration, is conceived here as an undivided unit. An illustration of a perceived instant occurs when one listens to a speedy typist, noting the rapid succession and variations in patterns of the sounds which struck keys make; but each such single sound is not perceived as divided. Those who believe that any experienceable unit of time can be mathematically divided infinitely until some indivisible infinitesimal is reached regard infinitesimal instants as unperceivable. But according to the view proposed, each kind of change requires its own kind of time to occur, and each unit of change and each eventity as a temporal unity has an undivided character about it. To the extent that an eventity is the same eventity from beginning to end, it is not divided by differences; to this extent it may be regarded as an instant.

However, an instant is always viewed as some smaller part of a larger context and so may be regarded as undivided from this external viewpoint. Just as eternality is here interpreted as undivided internality, so instantaneousness is here interpreted as undivided externality. In these senses the eternal and the instantaneous are the internal and external aspects of the undividedness of every eventity as a temporal whole. Instantaneity and eternality may be regarded as polar opposites characterizing every eventity as an undivided temporal whole. Thus we have another double-aspect dimension of the multiple aspect theory of the nature of time.

Other Theories of Time

The foregoing theses together constitute a hypothesis, or a theory, about time that differs from many other theories. My following summaries and examples must be regarded as merely approximations to theories actually held by proponents.

ONLY EVENTS EXIST; THERE IS NO DURATION. (a) According to the theory of infinite divisibility of any mathematically interpretable unit, whether of space or time, so that between any two points or instants there is another, ad infinitum, the ideal end product of such division is an infinitesimal point or instant, that is, one which has no extension or duration. If what is past does not exist and what is future does not exist so that only what is present exists, and if what is present is always such an infinitesimal instant, then it and nothing else exists. Each such instant is an event. Hence, there is no duration. All appearances of duration are illusory.

(b) Bertrand Russell, if I remember correctly, proposes (or at least supposes) that the universe exists for an instant, then does not exist for an instant, then exists for an instant, and so on. This theory holds that such events are even discontinuous with each other, in contrast with the usual mathematically postulated artificial continuum defined as between any two instants is another one. The miracles of instantaneous creation, instantaneous destruction, and instantaneous repetition of previous patterns, remain unexplained.

ONLY DURATION IS; THERE ARE NO EVENTS. In Hindu metaphysics, Shankara's *Nirguna Brahman*, the only ultimate reality, is timeless being.[4] All events are illusory (*maya*), because they appear to have a being and nature different from *Nirguna Brahman*; but reality is nondual (*advaita*), so apparent events have no reality apart from timeless Brahman. Strictly speaking, we cannot attribute duration or even timelessness to Brahman either, since it is entirely without attributes (*nirguna*). But it always is, not in the sense of "always" as "at all times" but in the sense that it is whether anything else is or not.

DURATION DEPENDS ON EVENTS; EVENTS DO NOT DEPEND ON DURATION. Events occur. Duration consists in the span between two or more events. If there were no events, there could be no duration. If somehow there were only one event that happened instantaneously, there would be no duration. Duration depends on the occurrence of two or more events that are related to each other successively. This is usually called "the relational view of time" and is contrasted with "the container view of time" to be discussed next. Gottfried Leibniz is usually credited with first stating "the relational theory of time."[5] See discussion of space which follows.

EVENTS DEPEND ON DURATION; DURATION DOES NOT DEPEND ON EVENTS. (a) Orthodox Christianity believes that an eternal (i.e., timeless) God existing prior to creation of the world and the creation of time, will also exist after the end of the world and the end of time. Time depended, depends, and will depend for its existence on being created and sustained in being by God who does not depend on created time for his own existence. All events occur within created time. Created durations also occur, but they may be regarded more as longer-lasting events within the dependent temporal existence.

(b) Plato, who influenced the Christian doctrine of time, postulated an eternal realm of pure and perfect ideas or forms that served as patterns used by the creator (*demiurgos*) in making men and things in the world. "Time is the moving image of eternity." Particular things behave temporally and imperfectly because the eternal forms are only imperfectly embodied in them.

(c) The Neo-Platonist philosopher Plotinus conceived ultimate reality as The One, utterly unrelated to the temporal universe that emanates from it. Levels of being emanating from The One degenerate from a highest level of being without parts, spatial or temporal, through the physical world's levels of increasing plurality of both spatial and temporal parts, toward a beingless void. Events, the shorter the less real, nevertheless do not lack reality, as with Shankara, but exist as less real than the nontemporal and as dependently real.

(d) Isaac Newton formulated the classical view of time as an absolute, independently existing, container. "Absolute, true, mathematical time, of itself, and from its own nature, flows equable without regard to anything external, and by another name is called duration."[6] Events happen in time. But time may be empty of events. If there were no time, or duration, within which events can occur, there could be no events. But there can be, and may well be, durations within which no events occur.

EVENTS AND DURATIONS BOTH EXIST BUT COMPLETELY INDEPENDENT OF EACH OTHER. Sankhya-Yoga philosophers divide ultimate reality into two completely different kinds of beings: First, *purusha*, pure timeless spirits; and, second, *prakriti*, evolving nature, which like Plotinus' creation devolves from quiescent duration through several stages of increasing activity and differentiation, both spatial and temporal. The minutest flick of action embodies *prakriti* in its most degenerate form. Accidental encounters between spaceless and timeless spirits and *prakriti* both lure it from quiescence into activity and create in the spirits a reflected illusion of existing actively and temporally. Yogic liberation of spirits from nature restores them to their nontemporal purity and returns nature to its quiescent state. Such quiescence is perfect, hence without events, except that the tendency toward action is perpetually present and is kept in check only by maintaining equalized tensions between the *gunas*, or forces existing as tendencies to act.

The temporary coincidence of timeless spirits and evolving *prakriti* (which enjoys an illusion of being conscious in the presence of spirits) in no way influences the nature of either. Neither depends on the other for its nature, although *prakriti* cannot activate its temporal processes, and thus events, except in the presence of spirits.[7]

EVENTS AND DURATIONS NEITHER EXIST NOR DO NOT EXIST. Madhyamika, or Sunyavada, Buddhists idealize ultimate reality as purified of all distinctions, including distinctions between events and duration, and time and timelessness. Ultimate reality is indescribable. But if we insist on describing it, we do so by asserting that it neither is A, nor non-A, nor both A and non-A, nor neither A nor non-A, thereby negating all negation and hence all distinction. If we persist and ask if it is temporal or timeless, we hear that it is neither temporal, nor nontemporal, nor both temporal and nontemporal, nor neither temporal nor nontemporal. Hence it neither occurs, nor endures, nor both occurs and endures, nor neither occurs nor endures. It is nameless, but we name it *sunya*, the void of all distinctions. Curiously the events and durations and all other distinctions appearing in our experiences, called "suchness," are also indistinct from *sunya*.[8]

Time and Other Categories

The foregoing sketch of theories of time leaves unexplored relations of the problem of time to other metaphysical and epistemological problems. Most obvious perhaps are relations of time and space, time and quantity (and measurement, both measurement of time and time as a measure), beginning and ending of time, finiteness and infinity, and the differing theories regarding them. Issues regarding whether time is subjective or real, or both, and in what ways, can hardly be understood clearly apart from other epistemological problems. And explorations of experiencing time deserve extensive treatment in their own right. If time is indeed a category of existence, then an adequate account of it will be incomplete until its relations to all of them are stated, and an adequate account of them will entail accounts of their relations to it.

12 / SPACE

Space exists. Existence is spatial. What is space? Answers range all the way from "nothing" ("nonbeing," Parmenides) to "everything," or at least "everything physical" (Descartes, "matter" = "extension"). Two kinds of views have predominated.

Container and Relational Theories of Space

The "container" view holds that space exists as a container that is empty until something is put in it. It exists whether anything is put into it or not. Some hold that such space is infinite, that is, that it has no outer limits. Some hold that such space is finite, that is, that if one goes in any direction (space has three dimensions), he will eventually come to the end of space, beyond which there is nothing, not even space.

The "relational" view holds that space is merely an external relation between things that coexist. Space is what is between things when there is nothing else between them. Whenever things exist, space exists between them; but whenever things cease to exist, then the space between them ceases to exist. If I put a ball in a box in my room, the ball is in the space in the box (i.e., between the walls of the box), and the box is in the space in my room (i.e., between the walls of my room). While the ball is in the box, I can observe the space between the surface of the ball and a wall of the box. When I remove the ball, that space is gone, even though the space between the walls of the box remains. Likewise I can observe the space between a wall of the box and a wall of my room; and I can take the box out of the room and ob-

serve that the space between the walls of the box and room is
gone, but the space between the walls of my room remains.

Aspectival Theory of Space

Can these two views, the container and the relational, be recon-
ciled? When stated in their extreme forms, they cannot. If "things
are in space" and therefore depend on space, there must be space
before there can be things. If "space is in things or in between
things" and therefore depends on things, there must be things
before there can be space. From a broader perspective, space and
things may be seen as supplementing and complementing each
other in ways in which they appear as mutually interdependent.

We may call this an "aspectival" theory of space, or, even better, a "multiaspect theory of space," including both relational and
container aspects. But space itself, as we shall see, is an aspect of
something else. Space, we propose, is a categoreal aspect of existence.

In discussing both the container and relational views of space,
we observed that things and space are opposed to each other.
Whether things are in space or space is in things, according to
these views, a space is not a thing and a thing is not a space. Yet
when we explore the matter further, we find that the situation is
much more complicated than either of these views recognize. For
relative to each thing there is both the space outside it, the space
between its outer limits, and the space between the things inside
it. So each thing functions in such a way that it is both a thing in
relation to other things, thereby contributing to constituting space
as a relation between it and other things, and a thing that contains
other things within it, thereby contributing to constituting space
as a container of the things within it.

Also the things inside of the thing are themselves interrelated
and related to it, thereby contributing to space as relational. More-

over, if anything is put into the space between the thing and the other things to which it is related, that space functions as a container and the thing thereby contributes to space as container. So both the space outside a thing and the space inside that thing may function either as relational or as a container or, probably most of the time, as both.

Furthermore, things and space interdepend. Each depends on the other. Without things there could be no space, and without space there could be no things. "Individuals and space presuppose one another. Without at least two individuals, there would be no space, and without space, individuals could not exist."[1] Space and things are opposites, but complementary opposites.

In the container view, things depend on space without space depending on things. In the relational view, space depends on things without things depending on space. The view presented here, however, is that space and things exist together in such a way that no new thing can come into existence without coming into existence in an already-existing space but that the already-existing space depends for its existence on being involved in a relation between still other already-existing things. And when a new thing comes into existence (in an already-existing space), it causes the emergence of new spatial relations with other things that did not exist before it existed. Thus in this sense each new space depends on one or more new things for its existence. There are no things that are not in space. There are no spaces that are not between things. Hence both the container and relational aspects are categoreal to existence.

Curiously, despite the seeming opposition between things and space, space may also function as a thing and a thing may function as a space. On the one hand, we have already seen how a thing may function as spatial in the sense that it contains parts that are themselves spatially related to each other and to it as a whole. As a whole of coexisting parts, the spatial relations between its parts are themselves parts of it. It is in part constituted by such spatial relations, and such space as it contains participates as ingredient constituents in its being and nature. Things function as spaces.

On the other hand, consider how space may function as a thing. Whenever spatial relations between things persist, both the things and the space function substantially. When this happens, we may then treat such spaces as themselves things. For example, the space in my mailbox functions as something I can rely on. I can talk about it and ask you to put a letter in my box. I can measure it and say that it will hold a package of a certain size. I may even say that it has the same size as the box next to it. When I do this, the partition between the spaces seems to function as a spatial divider between the spaces in the boxes, now talked about as if they were things. The seeming reality of such a space functioning as a thing gains in practical significance when I pay rent for the box, and similarly when I pay money for (the space in) my room, for cubic footage in a warehouse or office building, for a lot on which to build a house, or for the acreage needed for a farm. Spaces can function as things.

Consider a problem that bothers those who have studied space by studying geometry before studying metaphysics, or astronomy, or subatomic physics. Attempts to understand space abstractly, in terms of points, lines, planes, and cubes can yield an abstract exactness difficult to match in the existing world. The minutest particle that exists is still not a geometric point. It still has its own extension and internal space. In practice, measurements of the distance between two stars,[2] between two cities, between two houses, between two posts, or between two pins treat the stars, cities, houses, posts, and pins as "points," despite their own internal space. There is a sense in which each thing can be taken as a "point" in this sense. In this sense, the thing is viewed as a single entity, as a unit, as an individual. An individual, we find by looking in Webster's dictionary, is "an indivisible entity." To be individual is to be "existing as an indivisible whole."[3] As an individual, each thing is an undivided (even if not indivisible) whole, and as such functions as a point in space.

On the other hand, the same thing as a container of parts is an area, or rather a cube, with a volume and thus a space. Just as in exploring time we found instantaneity and eternality as the outer and inner aspects of the undividedness of an event, so we now find pointedness and volume as the outer and inner aspects of the undividedness of a thing as an individual or whole.

Space and Other Categories

SAMENESS AND DIFFERENCE. Things and space are different. Two or more things are different from each other as things. Two or more spaces are different from each other as spaces. Without difference we could have neither things, nor spaces, nor both things and spaces. So things and space depend on difference in order to be. Difference is a category of things and space as well as of existence generally.

Things and space are alike. Two things are alike in being things. Two spaces are alike in being spaces. Things and space are alike in that they are mutually dependent on each other for their existence and are thus alike in sharing such relation of mutual dependence. Things are like space in the sense that they contain the space internal to them within which their parts exist. Space is like things when it functions as a substantial container; this is especially obvious when it is rented or bought and sold.

CHANGE AND PERMANENCE. Space is an external relatedness of things that coexist. Merely by itself, the word "coexistence" does not mean that either change or permanence is involved. But if, or since, existence involves both change and permanence, existing space is involved in such change and permanence.

It is obvious that when any space (whether internal or external to a thing) remains the same through time, it is permanent. There are permanent spaces. And spatiality, as a category of existence, is a permanent aspect of existence.

On the other hand, when any thing changes in any way, then space (whether internal or external to that thing) also changes in the sense that it is now space relative to a changed thing. For example, if the thing shrinks, its internal space diminishes and its external space increases. If a new part is added to the thing, the spatial relations of that part to the other parts and to it as a whole enter into the constitution of its internal space, thereby changing such space in such a way as to include them. If the thing changes its external position, or has another thing come to be located near it, its external space changes in ways to accommodate the new position or thing. Spaces do change. New spaces come into being when new things come into being, and spaces related to things cease to be when those things cease to be. And change as a category of existence is thereby a category of all existing space.

TIME. Space and time are linked together so commonly that the temptation to treat them as apposite opposites is almost irresistible. Recent theories treating time as a "fourth dimension" of a "space–time" continuum yield mind-boggling conceptions. Nevertheless, although having certain utilitarian advantages, mathematical treatment of a four-dimensional space–time continuum seems to overlook some of the immeasurable complexities involved in existing space and time.

Space has three dimensions (or, if every diameter of a sphere is a dimension, an infinite number of dimensions) whereas time has only one (succession, or passage from past through present to future). But time involves not only events and duration but also an overlapping of presents of different lengths (e.g., present heartbeat, present day, present year, present century). So, although describing space in terms of the coexistence of two or more things seems simple enough, when we recognize how complex time is, space (or spaces) also appears to be amazingly complex.

When two events, such as the enrollment of my son and your daughter in the same college for one semester, both endure for a time, their spatial relations remain the same, relative to that event, for that semester. The multiplicities of shorter events, such as their having a one-hour class together, bumping into each other in the hallway, or glancing at each other in passing buses, have their own durations as coexistences and thus their own durations as spatial relations. So space conceived in terms of coexistence of things or events (eventities) is involved in all the complexities of time.

Since both space and time are here proposed as categories of existence, neither can exist without the other existing. Both are regarded as aspects of existence. Instead of thinking of time merely as a fourth dimension of a four-dimensional space–time continuum, I prefer to regard all the categories of existence as dimensions and all the complexities inherent in each category (such as the dimensions of space) as additional categories and thus additional dimensions of existence.

SUBSTANCE. Things are substantial to the extent that they remain through change. So also are spaces, both the space between one thing and another and the space inside each thing. Some spaces are more substantial than some things; for example, the space in my room is such that I can move something into it and then move it out again while the space in the room as a container remains the same; however, such space depends upon the substantiality of the walls. Some things are more substantial than some spaces; for example, I blow up a balloon, which involves a change in both internal and external space; I let the air out again, and the spaces change again; but the balloon, as a thing, remains the same, I presume. Substances are spatial to the extent that they coexist.

RELATIONS. Things are related, and minimally are both similar and different from each other. Spaces are related, and minimally are both similar to each other, at least in being spaces, and are different from each other, at least in being different spaces. Things and space are related and are both different from each other (each is not the other) and are also similar in the sense that a thing functions spatially and a space functions as a thing.

But relations are also things, for we can talk about marital relations, ecological relations, political relations, and so on as kinds of relations and as kinds of things. We can talk about "a relation" (noun) as well as two things "being related" (verb). And relations are also spatial whenever the relations between two or more coexisting thus also coexist. For example, the husband–wife relationships in two neighboring families coexist; hence these relationships, as well as the families, are spatially related.

UNIVERSALS AND PARTICULARS. The likenesses of two or more things are universals, and the likenesses of two spaces are universals. Space is a universal in the sense that all spaces are alike in being spaces. All are alike in involving coexistence of things. If there can be no things without space and no space without things, then the interdependence of space and things is itself a universal and, as a hypothesis proposed here, a category of existence. Each thing is a particular thing, and each space is a particular space, and each relation between a thing and its space is a particular relation. But also each particular is spatial, because it coexists with other particulars, both outside and inside itself. And each universal is spatial as long as it coexists with other universals. For example, a row of black fence posts, each topped with a white knob, embodies both the universal consisting of the likeness of the black color of the posts and the universal consisting of the likeness of the white color of the knobs; the two universals coexist in a spatial relation such that one is above the other.

Other Theories of Space

In addition to the container and relational theories already discussed, we mention views attributed to Parmenides, Newton,

Descartes, Leibniz, Bradley, Shankara, Kant, and S. Alexander.

1. Parmenides, famous for his statement that "being is; non-being is not," regarded space as nonbeing, and thus as being not. "Naught is or shall be other besides or beyond the Existent."[4]

2. Newton held space to be not only a container but also an absolute container. "Absolute space, in its own nature, without relation to anything external, remains similar and immovable. Relative space is some movable dimension or measure of the absolute spaces...."[5] When the earth moves on its axis, the space in my house moves around the earth, but absolute space remains unmoved.

3. Descartes, French "father of modern philosophy," said: "A space, or intrinsic place, does not differ in actuality from the body that occupies it.... In reality the extension in length, breadth, and depth that constitutes the space is absolutely the same as that which constitutes the body."[6] Matter and space are identical, and there is no empty space. But Descartes also held that matter is not all that exists, for spirit, mind, or consciousness also exists, and it is not spatial.

4. Leibniz, who held that space is "something merely relative" and "consists in relations," is credited with originating a relational theory of space, in opposition to Newton's absolute space. He concluded, however, that "space is itself an ideal thing."[7] As an idealist, he claimed there is no need for any real space corresponding to such ideals.

5. Bradley denied that space either has, or belongs to, reality, because "space is a relation—which it cannot be; and it is a quality or substance—which again it cannot be."[8] He argued that space is not a mere relation, because a space must consist of parts which are spaces which, taken as a collection, would be a collection of solids, which solids would not be mere relations and which collection as an interrelation would not be space. If space is taken as a whole, it is a substance that is clearly as solid as the parts it unites and thus is not a relation. Then he argued that space is

nothing but a relation, and then lengthily refuted this view with seeming evidence for the conclusion that "space is a relation between terms, which can never be found."[9] Space is mere appearance, even though it is not incompatible with his "Absolute."[10]

6. Shankara, Advaita Vedantist, held that Brahman is the only reality, that Brahman is nonspatial, that spatiality is a false appearance. "Space implies coexistence of a plurality of objects."[11] But Brahman, or reality, is one and indivisible. Therefore space is unreal.

7. Kant claimed that we cannot know the nature of things in themselves, but we do and must perceive things as spatial because spatiality is a necessary form of our way of perception. "Space is nothing but the form of all appearances of outer sense. . . . If we depart from the subjective condition . . . space stands for nothing whatsoever."[12]

8. Alexander, influenced by Einsteinian relativity theory, claimed that "the world does not exist in Space *and* Time, but in Space-Time." "There are no such things as points or instants by themselves. There are only point-instants or pure events. In like manner there is no mere Space or Time but only Space-Time. . . ." "Space-Time is the stuff of which matter and all things are specifications."[13]

13 / RELATIONS

Many kinds of relations exist. If the nature of a relation depends in any way on what it relates, then there are as many kinds of relations as there are kinds of things that are related. But, since they are all alike in being relations, do they not all have something in common? Our first question about relations is, then, "What is a relation?" or "What is it that all relations have in common?"

Difference and Sameness

Minimally, a relation involves two things (traditionally called "terms") that are related. The two must be different at least in whatever sense they are two. Thus, minimally, relation involves difference. But also the two must be alike in some sense, for in being related they at least have their relation in common. Even the relation of negation, wherein each of two or more things is not the other, involves the two negatively related things in sharing it in common. "As a relation, negation both unites and separates its terms."[1]

Hence, minimally, relation involves the things related in both some sameness and some difference. The amount and kinds of sameness and difference may vary from relation to relation; but if either all sameness or all difference ceases, relation ceases. "A 'relation' in which the terms are either totally different or totally similar is no relation at all."[2]

Relations and Other Categories

CHANGE AND PERMANENCE. If to change is to become different, then change is, or involves, a relation. For becoming different involves both a difference between two things (namely, the thing before it changed and the thing after it changed) and a sameness between two things (namely, the thing that changes). If to be permanent is to remain the same, then permanence is, or involves, a relation. For remaining the same involves both a sameness that remains and a difference between the two (or more) times from which and to which it remains. And change and permanence are related. For each is not the other and therefore is different from the other; yet both involve a same "it" which is, or has, both permanence and change.

TIME. Time involves at least events and durations. Every event involves change, and every duration involves remaining permanent. Thus an event is, or involves, the relation of difference, and a duration is, or involves, the relation of sameness. Simultaneity, two events occurring at the same time, involves the relation of sameness. Succession, one event occurring after another, involves the relation of difference.

WHOLES AND PARTS. If wholes are always wholes of parts and parts are always parts of wholes, then a whole and its parts are interrelated. A whole–part relation is obviously a relation. A whole and its parts (any one of them or all of them) are different; also a whole and its parts (any one of them or all of them) are the same in whatever sense they constitute an organic whole, that is, that which is the whole of both whole and its parts. The parts of each whole are also related to each other, both in the sense that each part is different from every other part and in the sense that each part is like every other part in being a part of that whole.

SUBSTANCE. If to be substantial is to remain the same through change, or to be permanent, and if a substance is anything which so remains, then substance involves the relation of sameness insofar as it is that which remains the same and the relation of difference insofar as such remaining involves remaining through different times. The more substantial anything is, the more it remains the same, that is, through more different times.

Not only do change, permanence, time, wholes, parts, and substance involve relations; relations themselves change, are permanent, come in wholes and parts, and are substantial. If a relation is complex, it has parts and thus there is also a whole of it. If one relation remains longer than another, it is more substantial. As we shall see, the same is true of the relation of relations to all other categories. All of them involve relations, and relations involve all of them.

Other Theories of Relations

Not all thinkers are willing to agree that every relation involves both some sameness and some difference between its terms. Some regard the ways in which the things related are different from, or other than, each other as more important. Others regard the ways in which they are alike, similar, the same, or identical as more important. These differing emphases tend to beget opposing views about the nature of relations. The first view, holding that relations separate or divide things from each other in such a way that they exclude each other, has come to be called the "theory of external relations." The second view, holding that relations unite things in such a way that their likeness is somehow a part of each thing, is called the "theory of internal relations." Now holders of these two views may differ with respect to how much difference or how much sameness is involved; but emphasis on the oppositeness of the two views tends to lead their holders to make extreme statements.

EXTREME EXTERNALISM.   This view holds that things that are

related are completely external to each other or are not each other. In order to be related, things must be different from each other. "The claim is sometimes made that terms are independent of relations, and not only of specific relations, but, it seems, of any relations at all."[3]

For example, a person and a table are different from each other, and the relation between them consists in such difference. The difference of the person from the table is not a part of the person and is not a part of the table; it is external to both. And the relation between them, consisting of this difference, is external to both. It consists entirely of what, or how, such differences are external to them.

EXTREME INTERNALISM. This view holds that things that are related are completely internal to each other, or are identical with each other. All are parts of the universe, which is a single whole, and are inseparable for it. Relations unite things; things that are divided are unrelated. When two things are related, they share the same relation; and, being the same, they are identical and not different. Since each thing is related to everything else in the universe, it is likewise united to all of them or shares sameness with all of them. And since the universe unites them all, they all share in this unity, which is one and hence completely internal. "External relations must be debarred from existing in the Absolute."[4]

For example, a person and a table, although seemingly different, are both integral parts of the universe, which is manifesting itself through them. It is only because they appear to manifest the universe in different ways that they appear different. The underlying basic unity of the universe consists entirely in internality.

MODIFIED EXTERNALISM. Things that are related are more external to each other than internal to each other. That is, although things that are related are both external to each other and internal to each other, they are more external than internal to each other. Relations between things separate them more than unite them or keep them apart more than bring them together. "There are degrees of internality, and complete externality is of the nature of a limit."[5]

MODIFIED INTERNALISM.   Things that are related are more internal than external to each other. That is, although things that are related are both internally and externally related, they are more internal to than external to each other. Every relation is more an internal relation than an external relation. In other words, relations between things unite them more than separate them, or bring them together more than keep them apart. "Every relation essentially penetrates the being of its terms and is in this sense intrinsical."[6] "A relation is not a thing stretching between two other things. . . . A relation is not between its terms but in its terms. Or, better, its terms are in it."[7]

EXTREME MIDDLISM.   Things that are related are exactly as much internal to each other as external to each other. Every relation is exactly as much an internal as an external relation. "Many relations divide as much as they connect."[8]

Many other theories about relations must be omitted here. Some would say that all relations are alike in being relations, and that they are neither internal nor external but only seem so. Others would say that there are two completely different kinds of relations, internal and external, which have nothing in common. But let us hope that "the present drift is decidedly toward the admission of both internal and external relations."[9] Or, better, that the drift is toward the view that every relation has both internal and external aspects.

Relation as a Category of Existence

An examination of the hypothesis that whatever exists is relational is not essential to a consideration of the nature of metaphysics but is proposed here for further consideration. Nothing exists without being related. No one thing is everything, so each thing is related, directly or indirectly, to everything else. Each thing is like everything else in existing and in embodying the categories of existence; it is in this sense internally related to everything else and is different from everything else in being itself, and in this sense it is externally related to everything else.

14 / UNIVERSALS

Probably no problem has troubled metaphysicians more than that of the nature and relations of universals and particulars. Solutions to so many other problems, including the nature of things, selves, societies, God, kinds, laws, minds, and ideas, depend on how universals and particulars are understood.

What Is a Universal?

When two or more things are alike, or are the same, in any way, that way in which they are alike is a *universal*. A universal consists of the likeness or sameness of two or more things in any respect.

The word "things" here is a completely general term denoting anything, or anything in any sense. Thus it includes events (or "eventities") and aspects. "Things" may be completely mind-dependent (e.g., occurring only in a moment of awareness) or completely independent of mind (i.e., unknown or even unknowable) or both (e.g., a thing in mind, or in awareness, may be like a thing which is not in mind or awareness). The words "alike," "like," or "same" are completely general terms with respect to what these likenesses are or may be (e.g., if there could be two nothings, that in which the two nothings were alike would constitute a universal). We could say that every similarity constitutes a universal, for by "similarity" we mean the same in some respect.

The term "universal" means "all." A universal consists of the likeness of all of the two or more things which are alike in some respect.

What Is a Particular?

A particular is a thing, any thing, in the foregoing sense. The meaning of the term "particular," when used as here in apposite opposition to the meaning of the term "universal," connotes oneness, unity, singleness, or individuality of a thing, and thus difference from other things; or that it is a thing that is different from other things. A particular (or particle) is a part of the whole, or all, of the two or more things that are alike in some respect. In this sense, a part, particle, or particular participates in a universal.

How Are Universals and Particulars Related?

Universals and particulars interdepend in several ways.

1. Each universal depends on its particulars for its existence and nature. A universal has no existence apart from its particulars. If all of the particulars on which a universal depends ceased to exist, that universal would also cease to exist, since any respect in which two or more particulars are the same ceases to exist when all of those particulars cease to exist. If some of the particulars on which a universal depends ceased to exist, then that universal would exist as something common to fewer particulars than it was before they ceased. It then depends on fewer particulars for its existence. When, relative to one particular that is in some respect unique, a second particular comes into existence embodying that same respect, the universal that emerges into existence thereby depends completely for its existence on those two particulars. When a third particular embodying that same respect comes into existence, then the universal is dependent for its existence on all three particulars as that which all three have in common. When many particulars embodying this universal come to exist, the universal depends on all of the many for its existence. But as the number of particulars increases, the dependence of the universal on each one

becomes less in the sense that one particular can cease to exist without the universal ceasing to exist (it ceases to exist merely as embodied in that one particular).

2. Each particular depends on a universal in which it participates for being the same as the other particulars which participate in that universal. Two or more particulars cannot exist as the same in some respect unless that sameness exists; that is, if there were no such sameness, two or more particulars could not participate in it. When many particulars embodying a universal exist, then another particular cannot come into existence and be the same as those particulars in the respect in question without thereby embodying the same universal.

When a universal depends completely on only two particulars for its existence, it is completely dependent for its existence on both of them, for if one should cease, it would cease. In such a case the universal seems more dependent on the particulars than the particulars are dependent on the universal. But when a universal depends for its existence on many particulars (especially when it depends on all other particulars, as is the case with all universals that are categoreal), then the universal seems more independent because, being less dependent on each particular for its continuing existence, it can survive the coming and going of various participating particulars. Then each particular functions as more dependent on that universal in the sense that such universal stands as something on which, or through which, each particular depends on all other particulars which are the same as it for such sameness.

If we think of any sameness in some respect as abstractable from the particulars and as having a kind of being independent of all such particulars, then the dependence of the particulars on the universal may seem less clear. In fact, once we conceive universals and particulars as completely independent of each other, we find it almost impossible to reunite them. Let us illustrate how a particular depends on a universal by a concrete example. Consider a mother, already having one child, giving birth to a second child. The sameness embodied in the two children by virtue of their being children of the same mother depends both on the continued existence of the mother (i.e., until the second child is born) and on the continued existence of the trait "being children of the same mother." Neither child can be what it is as a child of one mother without embodying in its existence its sameness with the other child in being a child of that mother. The first child exists as a particular in being the child of its mother before the second child is born. But it cannot exist as being the same as the second child until the second child exists and until the sameness in this respect (i.e., being children of the same mother) thereby exists also.

Hence, universals depend for their existence and nature on particulars in one way, and particulars depend for their existence and nature on universals in another way.

3. Each thing that is a particular embodies not merely one but many universals and depends on all of them in order to be what it is (i.e., for its existence and its nature). This kind of dependence is usually discussed in terms of "a thing and its properties" when the "properties" include universals. "There is a fundamental unity involved so that a thing has no existence apart from its properties and its properties no existence apart from a thing. In other words, a thing and its properties are inseparable."[1] On the one hand, a particular depends on whatever universals are embodied in it to constitute its nature and to this extent to determine its existence. On the other hand, if no universal can exist without being embodied in particular things, and if no particular thing can exist without embodying more than one universal, each universal then depends on all the other universals embodied in each particular thing which are necessary to the existence of that thing. In this way, universals depend on each other also to the extent that they

cannot exist in particulars in isolation from each other. But they depend upon the particular things in which they are embodied together for their existence as embodied and as interdependent.

Each particular not only depends on each universal embodied in it for part of its nature but also depends on all such universals for all of its nature except that part of it which is unique. And even its uniqueness involves a universal in the sense that, in order to be unique, a particular thing must embody uniqueness as something common to all unique things. Part of the uniqueness of each thing consists of the unique combination of universals embodied in it; in this sense even uniqueness is dependent upon universality.

Hence, in addition to the ways in which universals depend on particulars and particulars depend upon universals noted in 1 and 2 above, we here observe more complicated ways in which universals depend for their existence and nature on particulars and in which particulars depend for their existence and nature on universals.

Universals and Particulars as Categories of Existence

According to the hypothesis proposed here, existence involves both particularity and universality. Particularity is an aspect of every existing thing. Universality (i.e., being like other things in some ways) is an aspect of every existing thing. All the categories of existence are, of course, themselves universals; thus existence cannot have categories without having universals. But having universals is itself one of the categories of existence. And particularity, as a category (i.e., as something common to all existences) is thus itself a universal. All particulars are alike in being particular or in having particularity in common. But particularity exists only in particulars as something that is common to all particulars. Not only do universals and particulars interdepend; existence itself depends on, and interdepends with, both particulars and universals.

Universals and Other Categories

RELATIONS. How does the foregoing theory that particulars and universals interdepend in several ways relate to the theory that every relation has both internal and external aspects?

First, every universal is a relation: the relation of sameness or identity in some respect which any two or more particulars have in common. Each particular is a "term," and every universal is a relation between such terms. By internal relation and by internal aspect of relation, we mean whatever sameness exists between the terms related. Since a universal consists in the way in which two or more particulars are the same, the internal aspect of the relation between such particulars as terms is obviously taken care of. By external relation and by external aspect of a relation, we mean whatever difference exists between the terms related. Each particular that participates in a universal is different from every other particular that participates in that universal. The ways in which such particulars differ from each exemplify external relatedness between terms.

Furthermore, when several universals are embodied in a particular thing, they are all alike in being embodied in that particular thing. Such likeness exemplifies internal relatedness, even if of a seemingly lesser sort. Yet each such universal remains a different universal and hence retains external relatedness to all the other universals embodied in that particular.

In addition, the relation between universality and particularity involves both external and internal relatedness. They are externally related, because each is not the other. A universal is not its particulars, and the particulars in which a universal participates are not that universal. They are internally related to the extent that each is partly constituted by the other. Particulars involve universals in their nature by having universals as constituent properties or aspects, and universals involve particulars in their nature by having particulars as participants in them as what is common to these particulars.

Next, let us examine relations to see whether they exhibit universality and particularity. We have proposed that every relation has both internal and external aspects. First, to the extent that the two terms of a relation are alike in being related by that relation, such likeness constitutes a universal (as that which two or more things have in common). In this sense every relation, insofar as it is an internal relation, involves or embodies a universal. Second, to the extent that the two terms of a relation are different, they are externally related and do not embody universality, except perhaps in the sense in which they are alike in each being not the other or in being different from the other. Third, each of the two terms related functions as a particular. Fourth, every relation is a particular relation.

SPACE. Space, relative to things, has two aspects, relational and container. The relational aspect of space has been explored in principle in the preceding treatment of relations, except that if space involves, or consists of, "coexistent otherness" relative to any thing (i.e., the existence of other things *at the same time*), then an additional element of sameness, or universality, is involved. The things that are spatially related are particulars, but since as spatial they coexist, they are alike in coexisting and thus embody a universal constituted by such existing at the same time.

The container aspect of space exists between coexisting things, both when there is nothing else between them and when other things do exist between them. When other things do exist between them, these things may be spoken of as existing in the *same space*. Here space functions in another way as a universal, both in the sense that the space that these things occupy is the same space and in the sense that they are *in* such space, which being in such space functions as a trait common to them. However, when there is nothing between two coexisting things, such space can hardly function as a universal in this way, for since a universal is what is common to two or more things, where there are no things there can be nothing common to them and hence no such universal. (Problems concerning conceptual space in abstract geometry are not treated here. Problems regarding the relational and container aspects of space recur for geometers, but no connection exists between their conceptions and real spatial situations until they act to introduce new things into such real existing spatial situations.)

Thus far, we have been concerned with things as particulars and space as universal. But exemplified by squares on a checkerboard, drawers in a desk, rooms in a building, or buildings in a city, we can refer to each as a particular space. Each such space is different from the others. Hence we see that space functions both as universal and as particular.

Not only does space function both as universal and particular; there are ways in which both universals and particulars function as spatial. To the extent that two or more particulars *of any kind* coexist, they exist as spatial. To the extent that two or more universals *of any kind* coexist in two or more particulars, they exist as spatial. (Note that this statement does not assert that all universals of any kind which coexist are spatial, for two or more universals may function as different aspects of the same particular without being spatial except in whatever sense that particular itself is also spatial. All categories of existence coexist; when they coexist in two or more particulars, they are spatial; when they coexist in one particular in any sense in which it is not spatial, they too are nonspatial.)

TIME. As previously noted, time involves two aspects: events and duration. Each event is a particular event and is different from every other event. However, all events are alike in being events; hence the event character of all events constitutes a universal. Before and after an event occurs, that event does not endure. But while it is occurring, it endures long enough for it to happen. To endure is to remain the same through change. If something remains the same through change, that remaining the same involves sameness of two or more things (i.e., what existed before the change and what existed after the change), and such sameness of two or more things is a universal. In whatever sense an event is instantaneous, it occurs without enduring. In this sense no universality is involved. In whatever sense an event is eternal (i.e., remains the same without changing), it endures without occurrences. In this sense, no universality is involved, for without such occurrences there can be nothing common to such occurrences to constitute a universal. (Problems concerning abstracted conceptual time are not treated here.)

Each duration is also a particular duration. And all durations are alike in being durations and so involve durationality as a universal. The event and duration aspects of each eventity are different, and hence particular, aspects. But to the extent that they are different aspects of the same eventity, they are alike in being aspects of that eventity and thereby participate in an additional universal.

Not only does time involve universality and particularity, but also there are ways in which universals and particulars are temporal, that is, happen and endure. For example, one day two raindrops struck my head at the same time. Their likeness in striking my head at the same time thereby embodied a universal. But such a universal existed only momentarily. The universality consisting of what was common to the two events was itself an event, namely, the event of their common occurrence. Consider another example. My father had two hands from before birth until he died. The universality consisting of their being alike in both being his hands endured as long as he lived. The categories of existence (i.e., aspects that are common to all existents) endure as long as existence endures, presumably forever.

SUBSTANCE.   If universality consists in the sameness of two or more things or events, and if substantiality consists of remaining the same through two or more changes (events), then substantiality involves universality; that is, as remaining the same through change, substantiality involves universality. In this sense whatever is substantial is universal, and all substances are, or involve, universals. Each substance is also, of course, a particular substance.

On the other hand, whenever a universal remains the same through change, it functions substantially and, in this sense, is a substance. For example, a husband and wife are alike in being married to each other; they have a child and thus change from not having a child to having a child. Their likeness in being married to each other while they both continue to live constitutes a universal. This universal, in remaining the same before childbirth and after childbirth, is thereby substantial.

Hence, universals and substances interdepend. Every substance is universal in whatever sense it remains the same through change. Every universal is substantial in whatever sense it remains the same through change. However, to the extent that universals are merely spatial (i.e., consist of the likeness of two coexisting events in their nonenduring aspects), they are not substantial. Also, when a duration ceases, any universality consisting of that duration also ceases. When a universal that remains through change (i.e., is substantial) ceases to exist, its substantiality ceases also.

LEVELS AND HIERARCHY. 1. What is universal at one level functions as particular at another level. For example, the twins in your family may be born on the same day as the twins in my family. The twins in my family constitute a universal in the sense in which they are alike in being born of the same mother at the same time. The twins in your family constitute a universal in the sense in which they are alike in being born of the same mother at the same time. But also the twins in your family and the twins in my family together constitute a universal of twins born on the same day, unless, of course, there are still other twins born on the same day who also participate in this universal. But all these twins participate in still another universal consisting of all twins born at any time. And each twin also participates in that universal consisting of all babies born on a certain day and in that universal consisting of all babies born at any time.

Furthermore, not only is each of the twins in my family a particular, but also insofar as the "twins in my family" and the "twins in your family," previously referred to as universal, participate in the universal "twins born on that same day," they participate as particulars in that universal. Likewise, when "twins born on that same day," previously referred to as a universal, participate in the universal "twins born on any day," "twins born on that same day" functions as a particular when participating in the universal "twins born on any day." Hence what is universal at one level may function as particular at another level.

2. Each universal is something, or a thing, and hence is a particular (i.e., a particular universal). As a particular, it is like all other particulars in embodying particularity as a universal. As a particular universal, it is like all other particular universals in being both on the one hand, particular, and on the other, universal. That universal which consists of how all other universals are alike is in a sense a higher-level universal and thus stands higher in a hierarchy of universals.

ORGANICITY.   Each universal is a kind of whole in which all of its participating particulars are parts. Insofar as this is so, a universal as a whole is opposed to its particulars as parts, and the particulars as parts are opposed to the universal as a whole. Each is not the other. But also, there exists that which consists of both the universal as a whole and its particulars as parts. Traditionally such an existent has been called a "concrete universal." But just as that whole which includes both a whole and its parts may be called an "organic whole" or an "organism," so what has traditionally been called a "concrete universal" may better be thought of as a kind of organism and as embodying concrete universality or "organicity."

For example, each person is a particular which embodies something that all persons have in common, called "humanity." But all humanity and all of the persons who embody humanity as that which they have in common together constitute "mankind" (i.e., both all men and their humanity). So understood, mankind exemplifies, and participates in, organicity.

Other Theories of Universals

Among the issues dividing theories of the nature of universals is one that deals with the problem of which is more real or the more ultimate kind of being, universals or particulars. The following theories are stated as general types which may be exemplified by one or more particular theories.

ONLY UNIVERSALS EXIST; NO PARTICULARS EXIST. Although it seems dubious whether anyone could hold such a theory about existence as a whole, Plato is interpreted by many as supposing that universals (i.e., the eternal Ideas or Forms) subsist eternally. But particulars did not exist until the world was created by the Demiurge. Thus prior to the creation of the world only universals existed.[2]

ONLY PARTICULARS EXIST; NO UNIVERSALS EXIST. The world consists of many different things; each one is an individual or a particular thing or substance. In naming things, we could have one name for each thing, as we do with proper names for persons. But convenience dicates that we use the same name for different things which seem similar. That is, in dealing with one tree we adopt the term "tree," and then when dealing with another tree we do not adopt another word (we may run out of different kinds of sounds) but use the same word over again. Any word that is used as a name for two or more things thus serves as a universal. This theory is called *nominalism* (Latin for "name" is *nomen*): Universals consist merely of names thus used, and they do not exist either in things or in some eternal realm.[3]

UNIVERSALS ARE MORE REAL THAN PARTICULARS. Particulars depend on universals more than universals depend upon particulars. Let us consider two examples, Platonism and Thomism.

1. According to Platonism, the existing world consists of particular things, each of which is a thing of some kind, and which kind is an imitation of a perfect, universal Idea or Form presubsisting eternally. The Demiurge in "creating" the things in this world did so with the ideas as master patterns, but in each thing the ideal pattern is embodied only imperfectly. Without any pattern, or universal, no particular reproduction of it could be made. Thus particulars depend for their existence both on the universals as patterns and the work of the creating Demiurge. The eternal Ideas or Forms are the universals that do not depend on the particulars.[4]

2. According to Thomism, God is both pure form, omniscient in having all the forms (universals) eternally present in his mind, and also the creator of all existing forms or essences. ". . . essence signifies something common to all natures by which diverse beings are disposed in different genera and species, as for instance humanity is the essence of man. . . ."[5] Particular beings consist of both form (soul) and matter (body). Angels (each is a separate species in itself or a universal with no particulars) are more perfect in reality than men (each man being a particular member of the single species). Universals are more real than particulars because they are eternally real at least in the mind of God, and particulars depend on them and on God not only for their creation but for their continuation in existence.

PARTICULARS ARE MORE REAL THAN UNIVERSALS. Several noted thinkers appear to support this type of theory.

1. David Hume, skeptical of all knowledge of the real world, proposed an extreme empiricist theory of the origin of our ideas. They originate in "impressions," not merely sensory impressions but also those appearing as emotions and passions. Each such impression is a particular. "Ideas," he says, are "faint images of

these in thinking and reasoning."[6] "Since nothing is ever present to the mind but [impressions and ideas], and since all ideas are derived from something antecedently present in the mind; it follows that it is impossible for us so much as to conceive or form an idea of anything specifically different from ideas and impressions."[7] Such ideas, at least those which serve as general ideas as a consequence of our using them habitually, to that extent are universals. However, because of the tenuousness of such universals, all existing only in minds as changeable habits, Hume has been called a "nominalist."

2. John Dewey, presupposing ideals about nature evolving through struggles for existence and survival of the fit, interpreted ideas as tools useful in adaptation and problem solving. Existing and thinking are processual, and each problematic situation is particular and must be solved in its own way. However, to the extent that experience reveals ways of adaptation that have worked before, one tends to try them again to determine whether or not they work now. Those which work again may be regarded as universals. Many do work again and again, as evidenced by the evolution of language, customs, science, and technology. ". . . universals have their place, but that place is to better approximation to what is unique and unrepeatable."[8]

3. Henri Bergson conceived ultimate reality as an enduring flux of personal experience (*élan vital*). The flux is a perpetual flow of living novelties of immediately intuited particularities. The intellect, in seeking to understand the flow, tries to capture it in fixed and static concepts which, though universal in the sense of capturing likenesses, are dead husks. "The intuition of duration [i.e., the flux of experience], when it is exposed to the rays of the understanding, . . . quickly turns into fixed, distinct, and immobile concepts."[9] The particulars, intuited in and as the flux of experience, are alive and thus more real. Universals as stoppages abstracted from the flux, although useful in science, technology, business, and engineering, are derivative, artificial, and dead.

4. Selecting Sartre's oft-quoted phrase, "existence precedes essence,"[10] we mention only that each act of will (*existence*) freely chooses to want what (*essence*) it wants to become. What (essence) it chooses depends on it as chooser (existence). Whatness (essence) as universal depends for its being on being chosen by a will (particular). An ideal of "authenticity" can be interpreted as the quality of a particular will when it refuses to have any essence (universal) imposed upon it from outside (e.g., from laws of society, laws of nature, laws of logic, from other wills, such as parents or police, or even from one's own previous promises). Spontaneity of each particular will is the ultimate reality, and what (any universal) is willed is a dependent result.

BOTH UNIVERSALS AND PARTICULARS EXIST, BUT THEY ARE ENTIRELY DIFFERENT IN NATURE. Four thinkers may be interpreted as approximating this type. All agree, however, that universals and particulars may cooperate in constituting actual existence.

1. Immanuel Kant, agnostic about the nature of things in themselves and about minds in themselves, concluded that what appears in experience results from two fundamentally different kinds of contributions, sensations (which provide particularity) and concepts (which provide universality). "To neither of these powers may a preference be given over the other. Without sensibility no object would be given to us. Thoughts without sensory content are empty, intuitions [i.e., of sensations] without concepts [i.e., universals] are blind."[11] Sensations and concepts are utterly unlike each other; yet both are necessary ingredients in our knowledge of objects in our phenomenal world.

2. George Santayana, more poetic than dogmatic in his philosophical commitments, proposed a picture of our world in terms of four "realms of being," the realms of "essence," "matter," "truth," and "spirit."[12] Two of these realms consist of universals and particulars, essence and matter. "The principle of essence is identity: ... each essence [is] a universal; for being perfectly self-contained and real only by virtue of its intrinsic character, it contains no

reference to any setting in space or time, and stands in no adventitious relations to anything. Therefore without forfeiting its absolute identity it may be repeated or reviewed any number of times." "Physical obstacles to exact repetitions or reproductions do not affect the essential universality of every essence, even if by chance it occurs only once, or never occurs at all." "The realm of matter ... is the field of action." The parts of matter are particular in the sense that all "are external to one another."[13]

3. Bertrand Russell asserted: "We have a division of all entities into two classes: (1) particulars, which enter into complexes only as the subjects of predicates or the terms of relations, and, if they belong to the world of which we have experience, exist in time, and cannot occupy more than one place at one time in the space to which they belong; (2) universals, which can occur as predicates or relations in complexes, do not exist in time, and have no relation to one place which they may not simultaneously have to another." "My own opinion is that the dualism is ultimate."[14]

4. Alfred North Whitehead distinguished "two ultimate classes of entities, mutually exclusive. One class consists of 'actual entities,' which ... are mis-described as 'particulars'; and the other class consists of forms of definiteness, here named 'eternal objects,' which in comparison with actual entities are mis-described as 'universals.' "[15] "An actual entity cannot be described, even inadequately, by universals; because other actual entities do enter into the description of any one actual entity. Thus every so-called 'universal' is particular in the sense of being just what it is, diverse from everything else; and every so-called 'particular' is universal in the sense of entering into the constitutions of other actual entities."[16] Whitehead's Philosophy of Organism regards universals and particulars as interdependent in constituting the actual world; yet his "eternal objects," somewhat like Plato's Ideas, subsist eternally prior to their "ingression" into "actual occasions."

NEITHER UNIVERSALS NOR PARTICULARS EXIST, EXCEPT AS ILLUSORY ASPECTS. Three theories, all Indian in origin, expound a common ideal in somewhat different ways. For Advaita Vedanta, *Nirguna Brahman*, for Madhyamika Buddhism, *sunya*, and for Theravada Buddhism, *bhavanga*, are being in which no distinctions exist. Regarding the distinction between universals and particulars, ultimate reality may be said to be neither universal, nor particular, nor both universal and particular, nor neither universal nor particular. Whatever distinctions may appear in *maya*, suchness, or *citta*, respectively, must be regarded as illusory. These may be described as "real illusions," since what appears in these illusions functions as having all the seeming power of the forces manifest in our experiences. But in ultimate reality, they have no distinct being.[17]

BOTH UNIVERSALS AND PARTICULARS ARE ASPECTS OF SOMETHING EXISTING AS MORE REAL THAN EITHER. Georg W. F. Hegel, an Absolute Idealist, whose intricate writings seem virtually unintelligible to beginners, may be interpreted as holding that all particular men together with the universal ("manness"), constitute a totality, "mankind," which is a "concrete universal." Although particulars and their universal are antitheses, they are *aufgehoben* (gathered up and preserved) in a synthesis which is more inclusive, and thus more real, than either alone. Either alone is an abstraction. A particular man who does not embody manness would be a nonexisting abstraction; and manness apart from all men is an abstraction. The concrete reality, mankind, which exists in and as individuals, embodies both manness (that which is universal in the sense that it is what is common to all men) and John Smith, Sumitra Krishna, and Mao Tzu as particular persons.

15 / ACTION

Action is both very simple and very complex in nature. On the one hand, that which is common to all actions is simple, even if being complex in some way is one aspect of that simplicity. On the other hand, actions are of such diverse and complex sorts that, until one comprehends many of the ways in which actions exist, his understanding of the nature of action will be inadequate. In what follows, we explore the nature of action by relating it to being, agency, function, actuality, inaction, and passivity.

Being

To act is to be. To be is to act. By these two statements I do not mean that "being" and "acting" are synonyms but only that no action can be without being, and that no being can be without acting as a being. That is, being and acting interdepend. How do being and acting differ? Although we may grammatically say that being is what is denoted by nouns and acting is what is denoted by verbs, what as metaphysicians we should mean is that both nouns and verbs have developed in our language because being and acting persist as distinguishable aspects of existence as experienced. Hence there are at least as many kinds of acting as there are verbs and tenses of verbs.

Some theorists hold that a thing must first be before it can act, or that being is ontologically prior to action. Others hold that action is prior to being, since a being can come to be, or can come into being, only by action; and can continue to be, or can continue in being, only by acting as continuing to be or through the action of continuing. But since *being* is a way of acting and *acting* is a way of being, acting and being interdepend. There can be no acting without the being of the acting, and there can be no being without acting as being.

Agency

Can there be action without an actor or an actor without action? Does action require agency; can there be an agent or actor which does not act? What is an agent? An agent is that which acts, or a thing which acts.

Some theorists believe that there must first be an actor before there can be action. Only an actor can act, they say; if there is no actor there can be no action.

Other theorists (e.g., pragmatic behaviorists such as John Dewey) hold that "a thing is what a thing does." That is, existence is a dynamic process in which actions occur. It is by observing activities and then inferring that, since there can be no action without an actor, there must be an actor involved in the action. But the actor, or thing which acts, depends on the action and its continuation, whereas the action does not depend on an actor. Action enacts agency which is more apparent than real, because it is completely dependent on the action, whereas thought tends to reify it, regarding it as real and action as dependent on it.

The view presented here holds that action and actor interdepend. There can be no action without an actor, and there can be no actor that does not act. But, although each is prior in its own way, each depends on the complementary contribution of the other in the act–actor or action–agency situation. There can be no action without a thing that acts; but no thing can be without acting, including acting as a thing.

Function

To act is to function and to function is to act. But functioning is a way of acting. To act is always to act in some way. No mere, bare, or pure activity exists. (Aquinas' "God as pure act" is a fiction.) Hence acting involves functioning, that is, acting in some way rather than merely acting without acting in any way. Thus action and function interdepend. How anything functions in any way depends on its nature. Different kinds of things have different natures and thus function in different ways. Different schools of thought describe the nature of things differently and thus have different conceptions of the way things function. For example, a school of anthropological thought called "Functionalism" claims as a "premise of the functionalist position . . . that no human custom, institution, or set of behaviors exists *in vacuo;* there must always be an interplay between the component elements of a social system, and a continuing interdependence between them is created on many different levels."[1]

Actuality

Action is temporal. Only what is present is actual. We distinguish between potential and actual, or between the power to become and what has become or has come into being. What is present may also be potential or have potentiality relative to the becoming of something in the future. But what will become in the future is not yet actual and thus is not yet in action. What is past has ceased to be present because it has ceased to be active. When we say that something "is actually past," we mean that its actuality has ceased. But actuality consists of action or, rather, in the acting, the actor, and what is being acted or enacted. Agency itself can be only by being actual. "Every agent acts according as it is actual."[2]

We may note, without exploring details, that since some events take longer to happen than others and some presents are longer than others, what is actual relative to one present is longer than what is actual in others. Since action and actuality interdepend, and since actuality and the length of presents interdepend, action interdepends with and varies with presents of different lengths. The implications of such intricacies stagger the imagination. Yet seemingly existence itself exists in all its intricacy without being bothered except as existence manifests itself in such imagination.

Inaction

If to be is to act and to act is to be, then to be inactive, that is, completely inactive, is not to be. When we speak of some being as inactive, we refer to its being inactive in some way. Only a being can be inactive in some way. "Being and action are inseparable.... To be is to act; the inactive is the non-existent."[3] "... the opposition is not between action and its opposite but between two different kinds of doing. 'The busy man is active, the idle one does nothing' we may legitimately say in ordinary conversation; but we do not mean that the idle man has stepped outside the sphere of action altogether.... Although he is idle and inactive, he is still doing something; he is lying down, it may be, or taking a stroll." "... inactivity is a form of action...."[4]

Passivity

Not only may two kinds of action, namely, acting on and being acted on, or acting as agent and acting as patient, be distinguished, but also both, like all of the foregoing aspects of action, may be regarded as categories of existence. Although, in one sense, being acted on by something else is different from and opposed to acting upon something else, in another sense acting as a recipient of action is acting just as much as acting as an agent. Both are ways of being. No thing can be acted on without being and without acting a being. Hence, in this sense, all patiency involves agency. Furthermore, as we shall see in exploring causation, unless something can be totally uncaused and totally without effect, no event or thing can fail to function both as patient and agent.

16 / PURPOSE

Is existence purposive? Some say yes. Some say no. Some say partly yes and partly no.

What is purpose? Purpose is easy to discuss at the human level. There we find two kinds: external and internal. What is the purpose of this typewriter? Its purpose is to serve my interest in typewriting. Its purpose is external to it and internal to me. What is the purpose of my life? To grow, to satisfy desires, and to be happy. Such purpose of my life is internal to me. I can ask whether my parents had a purpose in having me as a child. If they answer yes, then I am serving a purpose external to me and internal to them. Some things, at least, have both internal and external purposes.

Let us now inquire what is the minimum condition for the existence of purpose, how it is related to some other categories, and whether it exists categoreally.

Aim and Goal

Purpose in its simplest form is not completely simple but contains within itself a polarity. Each purpose involves both an aim and a goal. Aim and goal are different, but they are different ends of the same polarity. Sometimes when we ask about your purpose, we say, "What is your aim?" Sometimes when we ask about your purpose, we say, "What is your goal?" Aim and goal are so close together in purpose that we usually neglect to recognize that purpose is polar and involves both of these as poles.

Presumably, whatever exists as purposive is incomplete, for as long as there is a goal aimed at, such goal has not yet been attained. Although we may say that something has attained its goal, and thus was purposive, when we speak of something being purposive, we regard it as actual and active and moving toward its goal. To be purposive is to have direction. To be purposive is to be going from something to something. Thus purposive action involves change.

But, we may ask, may not something that has attained its purpose continue to be purposive? The purpose of this leg was not only to hold up this table but also is to hold up this table and will continue to be to hold up this table. Having achieved its purpose in the past does not prevent it from achieving its purpose in the present and from continuing to achieve its purpose in the future. But when such a seemingly static way of serving a purpose continues temporally, such purposive action involves a change in time. Legs are sometimes removed from tables and cease to serve their function. Only by continuing through changing times to serve their functions do they continue to be purposive.

Things differ relative to purposiveness. Some seem to be more purposive internally and some more externally. Some seem to embody a single purpose and some many purposes. Some seem very goal bound while others seem more urgently aiming. Some fulfill their purposes quickly; others persist purposively enduringly. Some seem to have rigidly fixed purposes while others are very flexible. Some things have purposes that demand perfection, and thus cessation of their being, while others have purposes which evolve through transformation into other purposes in ways that avoid final completion. Each thing has its own purpose, or purposes, that involve its own uniqueness, in addition to being interrelated with other things and their purposes. Purpose is something so simple that it is present in every change, so intricate that men, atoms, and galaxies can exist interdependently, and so comprehensive that we may meaningfully ask, "Does the universe have a purpose?"

Purpose as a Category of Existence

"No realm of being is devoid of purpose."[1] "All that is moved must have a goal towards which it is moved."[2] Purpose is present in greater or less degrees and may pass from a minimum to a maximum."[3]

Purpose and Other Categories

CHANGE. Although it may be obvious that purpose involves change, does change always involve purpose? If purpose means something that is intended by a mind, then probably our answer must be no. But if purpose minimally involves change with direction, then, since every change, as the becoming of a difference, involves going from something that is not to something that is, or from something that is to something that is not, or both, we can interpret the tendency to go from as "aim" and that to which the change goes as the "goal." If we can do this, then every change is purposive in this minimal meaning of "purpose." "Change ... must be teleological."[4]

WHOLES. If each existing thing is both a whole and parts, as we have proposed, do the parts serve the whole or does the whole serve the parts? If whole and parts interdepend organically, then each (whole and parts) serves the other and is served by the other. Here purposiveness is seen as very complicated so that even the simplest whole–part situation actually involves many interrelated purposes, especially when each thing as a whole is seen as a part of larger wholes and each part is seen as a whole with its own parts. The more interdependent things become, the more there is something in each, including each part and whole, which is an end or goal served by more other things as well as something in each which aims to serve ends in the others.

TIME. If events and durations are the parts and wholes of time, then time too is purposive or, rather, things that are temporal are purposive even as temporal. If each thing that exists is temporal (i.e., depends on all the events that constitute it as an enduring whole and exists as an event in its coming into being, remaining the same throughout its being, and going out of being), then the purposiveness of things can be seen to interdepend with the events and durations, or the temporal parts and wholes, of those things. Although we can differentiate between aim and goal in an event (i.e., the beginning of its being and the completion of its being), the purpose of the event has a unity about it, such than its aim is nothing apart from its implicit goal and its goal is nothing if not already something aimed at.

But events do not exist in isolation. We may observe purpose within a heartbeat, an orgasm, and a lifetime. But we may observe also that an orgasm is served by a heartbeat and serves a lifetime. But even such observations are too simple, for all are interinvolved with biological processes, human and animal, which may be thought of as the events of human and animal life in the existence of the universe. "By purpose, in its most general and unspecialized sense, we mean the interfitting or the constituent parts of any realm of being into a coordinated whole. The ontological meaning of purpose, in other words, is organic coordination."[5]

When longer-ranging events contain and depend upon shorter-ranging events, the unitary power of the event, or thing (eventity), as a whole provides a basis for its purposiveness in such a way that the parts seem to serve the whole and such that the future completion of that whole has some causal influence on the existence and cooperative behavior of such parts. Parts so influenced may thus have their present behavior determined in part by the goal aspect of the purposive nature of the larger whole. When goals are interpreted as ends, either as ends in themselves or as intrinsic values, such goals may seem to have a drawing power, a lure, even a causal power, to prompt efforts to achieve them. Whether larger wholes have more such drawing power or more such pur-

posiveness than smaller wholes, I cannot say. I speculate that sometimes larger and more complex and sometimes smaller and simpler
wholes are more powerful, or more purposive, as units of being.

Other Theories of Purpose

GOAL PRECEDES AIM. Sometimes we discover something that
we did not know existed, but the moment we see it we want it.
It, our goal, existed before we wanted it, aimed at it. Plato depicted the perfect forms of things as Ideas, or ideals, subsisting in
an eternal realm. These are our goals. We may discover them
embodied imperfectly in particular persons or horses or trees. But
these perfect ideas are our preexisting goals. Orthodox Christianity
depicts God and Heaven as eternal, and men as created for the
purpose of serving God, but also thereby serving themselves by
entering a preexisting Heaven where joy is perpetual.

AIM PRECEDES GOAL. Sometimes after a restful sleep we arise
with superabundant energy to do something without having yet
decided what to do. Let us say it is time for play, but I find others
still asleep. So I consider shooting baskets or batting tennis balls
against the house. But both would make noise and awaken others.
So I decide to jog and then skip down the sidewalk, something I
do not do when others are around. My aim, to play something,
preceded my actual goal, skipping down the sidewalk.

John Dewey depicted life as perpetual problem solving and each
new problem as presenting the need and aim for solving it. One
does not know what the solution will be, and hence what his goal
is, until he has worked at the problem. But his aim, to solve the
problem, is present from its beginning. For Dewey, the goal is an
"end-in-view" that continues to depend on the view or perspective
or aim of a person working toward it.

In contrast to both foregoing views, I have proposed that aim
and goal arise together, even though sometimes the one and some-

times the other is primary. In some purposive activities, the emphasis may shift more from aim to goal (we may become more concerned about the goal as we approach it closer) or more from goal to aim (we may become unsure of our goal and reconsider what we want). Sometimes aim and goal are rigidly interlocked right from the beginning. Sometimes the goal is clear but our aim unsure. Sometimes our intentions are clear, but what we are looking for keeps evading us. Sometimes our aims are flexible (anything interesting will satisfy) and our goals are fluid (happy faces, tasty foods, games at a party all please us). May not similar aim–goal variations prevail throughout existence?

PURPOSES ARE EXTERNAL. At least the purpose for which a thing came into existence is more fundamental than any purposes which may thereafter arise within it. Just as we make chairs, houses, watches, and automobiles to serve our needs, so we as persons, animals, plants, the earth, and the stars were made by God to serve his purposes. We may develop purposes of our own, but if they do not accord with the purpose for which we were made, we will suffer.

PURPOSES ARE INTERNAL. At least the most fundamental purpose of each thing is to be found not outside itself but within its own nature. The purpose of a tree is to grow to its fullness and produce other trees, not to be made into a table. The purpose of a cow is to grow to maturity and have calves, not to serve as beef. The purpose of a person is to develop his own potentialities to their fullest, not to serve in an army as a dictator's expendible. If there is a God, is not his own purpose internal to himself, rather than that of serving as a means to salvation of (i.e., serving the purposes of) other beings, such as men?

In contrast to these views, I have proposed that internal and external purposes may be equally significant, equally actual, and equally owned by a person or thing. Granted that sometimes internal purposiveness primarily preoccupies a person, as when crippled by indecision he struggles to make up his mind, at other times external purposiveness predominates, as when a person is campaigning for the presidency or other public office. Even though sometimes internal and external purposes seem to be in conflict, a person is more intelligent when the two not only interdepend but blend in ways in which both enrich and extend the other.

Hasserot said that "The direction of purposiveness is ... from the dependent to the independent."[6] But purpose may go in either direction and is better, in persons at least, when it can go in either direction, or in both directions at once, for interdependence, involving both some independence and some dependence, is richer than either alone. (Hasserot expressed this same idea as "organic coordination" in a previous quotation.[7])

No Purpose Exists.   Existence, whether completely mechanical or wholly or partly a matter of chance, has no purpose. Nothing happens without being caused to happen in the way it does happen. If purposes appear in some minds, they are merely illusions.

Existence, as *Nirguna Brahman* of the Advaitins or *bhavanga* of the Theravadins, is completely purposeless. Each, being without distinctions, has no distinction between aim and goal. Each, being self-sufficient, aims at nothing. If purposes appear, as *maya* or *avidya*, they are illusions arising from ignorance.

17 / INTELLIGENCE

Interpreting "intelligence" to mean ability to attain one's end or ends, we raise the question of whether intelligence is a metaphysical category. But first we should understand more fully what is meant by "ability to attain one's end or ends." Each thing has its own nature. This includes its being the kind, or kinds, of thing it is. Whatever its nature, its end is to fulfill that nature, to realize it by actualizing its potentialities. The natures of some things are very simple, others complex; some are fixed, others flexible; some are short, even instantaneous, others long-enduring, even everlasting; some have limited capacities, others have capacity to develop new capacities. Thus there are as many kinds of intelligence as there are kinds of things or natures.

The Meaning of Intelligence

Three problems remain to grapple with before we understand intelligence. The first pertains to survival and adaptation, the second to internal and external aspects of each nature, and the third to whether completeness or incompleteness is better.

SURVIVAL THROUGH ADAPTATION? Evolutionary doctrines of biological struggles for existence and survival of the fit may be extended to all existing things. But the definition of "intelligence" as the ability to adapt to relatively new situations needs to be revised, since some things find themselves in relatively unchanging situations, and what cannot adapt to the unchanging will fail to survive just as surely as what cannot adapt to the changing. So intelligence is the ability to adapt,[1] and the test of adaptation is survival long enough to achieve one's ends.

At the human level, intelligence is often identified with problem-solving ability, since survival depends on confronting and solving many different kinds of problems. The sciences are part of our intelligence if they help us to survive; but if they hasten our destruction, they contribute to our unintelligence.

Survival through adaptation is essential to the realization of our ends, for one fails to attain his ends if one does not survive long enough to actualize them. But it is not survival merely, which constitutes intelligence, but fulfilling one's nature to its fullest.

INTERNAL OR EXTERNAL? Intelligence is something internal, according to the Chinese philosopher Lao-tzu. "Each thing which grows and develops to the fullness of its own nature completes its course by declining again in a manner inherently determined by its own nature. Completing its life is as inevitable as that each thing shall have its own goal. Each thing having its own goal is necessary to the nature of things."[2]

Each nature, tao, is good, and action in accordance with it is good. So it is good to be born, good to be young, good to be old, and good to die. Each tao that lives each stage in its development naturally has intelligence, teh. But when the young try to be older and the old younger, they act unintelligently because they are acting against nature. ("What is against Nature dies young.")[3]

But unless one is a very simple kind of being, there is more to intelligence than achieving one's own merely internal ends. Most things do not exist in isolation but in interaction with other things, higher-level things of which they are parts, lower-level things which are parts of them, and other same-level things often of many different kinds. Even if one is not "an immortal Shakespeare," he leaves some influences on others after he dies. Physicists say that for every action there is an equal and opposite reaction and that some actions seem to produce an unending series of effects. In our later discussion of causation and creation, we shall try to show how new emergents in each nature may cause the world to become perpetually different.

To the extent that each thing has a part of its nature interdependent with the natures of other things, that part of its fulfillment (and thus of end or ends, which finds fulfillment in and through them) has part of its intelligence exercised through others. Whether we should call this external to the thing or extend our concept of what is internal to a thing to include its spreading persistence throughout the universe even after it has otherwise ceased to exist may be a verbal matter. But surely such fulfillment is external in the sense that it depends on being fulfilled in and through other things.

Lao-tzu was able to idealize each nature as being able to fulfill itself because he regarded each nature as in harmony with Nature. The philosophy of Confucius, otherwise largely in agreement with that of Lao-tzu, provided for the Chinese a counterbalance to Taoism's overemphasis on innerness. For Confucius, "Great wisdom consists in fully perfecting intelligence, in restoring morale to the people, and in attaining the highest good."[4] But his outline of steps to attain the goal does not stop until there is "established moral order in their states."[5]

Those who see things as existing more interdependently tend to find intelligence not merely internally and externally but also, or even especially, in the interactions between things (or in what John Dewey calls "transactions," whereby each exchanges with the other something which the other needs and can use for its own purposes). Where growth, development, and self-actualization of intricate potentialities are possible, the more intricate, even if not intimate, varieties of cooperation and interaction are needed for intelligent achievement. "Intelligence is a change that involves a mutual reorganization, an adjustment in the organism and a re-constitution of the environment."[6]

COMPLETE OR INCOMPLETE? What is the end of each thing?

We may distinguish two types or aspects of intelligence: that which achieves its end completely and ceases to be, and that which, while completing itself partly, remains incomplete but remains in existence. The issue at stake is whether it is better (i.e., more intelligent) to attain one's end completely and perfectly, so that there is no more for one to attain, or to attain one's end incompletely and imperfectly, so that one must go on living, that is, continue in existence, because part of one's end has not yet been attained.

To use an analogy, is that candy better which, when you eat a piece, satisfies you so completely that you do not want more or that which, when you eat a piece, not only satisfies you but also arouses in you an appetite so that you feel that you must have more? Which kind of nature is better, that which aims to perfect itself and to cease to be or that which aims to remain imperfect and to continue to be? I suspect that we will decide that it is not intelligence as such that will decide which is better, but that when our natures call for completion, intelligence will bring it about; and when our natures remain with uncompleted ends, intelligence will help them to continue longer until completion is finally achieved.

And to the extent that there are some natures which both perfect themselves in some ways and continue to perfect themselves in still other ways (for example, a flower or tree that blossoms or bears fruit only once and then dies versus a flower or tree that blossoms or bears fruit again and again for several years), we may judge these to have better natures. But the intelligence required for more complicated kinds of natures may be more difficult to sustain, partly because it tends to require an environment of other congenial and cooperative natures.

Unintelligence

What is the opposite of intelligence? Does intelligence have an apposite opposite? If intelligence is ability to achieve one's ends through adapting, then inability to achieve one's ends, resulting from inability to adapt, is unintelligence. Unintelligence may also characterize both the internal and external and the complete and incomplete, as well as their interdependent aspects of achieving ends.

Is unintelligence also a category of existence? If any existing thing does attain all its ends completely and is thus completely intelligent, unintelligence is not a category of existence. But if attaining all its ends completely means that it ceases to exist, it is completely nonexistent. If it continues to exist in any way, then there is more of it being embodied in other things on which it depends for further achievement of its ends as involved in such existence. By conceiving existing things as interdependent (i.e., as partly independent of and partly dependent on each other), the view presented here holds that things are partly intelligent and partly unintelligent, because each can attain some of its ends completely but others only incompletely. If this is so, then both intelligence and unintelligence are categories of existence.

We have not explored the nature of kinds, each of which has its own kind of ends, and thus of intelligence and unintelligence, but we hold that things of each kind also are more or less intelligent. Part of the motive which some philosophers have for idealizing some, if not all, things and kinds as perfect, or at least perfectible, and thus endowing them with timeless being, is the desire to eliminate unintelligence as a category of existence. To hold that a thing has achieved its ends completely and that it continues to exist, where existence involves time and the continuing emergence of at least new temporal ends, is to be involved in a contradiction. By postulating the ideal of eternal being, that is, being with all ends achieved and hence uninvolved with temporal incompleteness, one can escape this contradiction.

Intelligence and Other Categories

SAMENESS.   Intelligence is the ability to remain the same when survival and attainment of ends requires such remaining the same and is the ability to become different when survival and attainment of ends requires such becoming different. Adaptation involves both some remaining the same and some becoming different; so intelligence involves both.

WHOLES.   An organism, consisting of both a whole and its parts, survives and perishes and realizes ends while surviving. Which end, or ends, does intelligence serve, that of the whole or those of the parts? Some organisms are more mechanical, wherein the parts seem to have more stability, and some are more "spiritual," wherein the whole seems to predominate. So it may be that in some kinds of things intelligence serves the parts more than the whole, and in others intelligence serves the whole more than the parts. But, according to this view, even though such imbalance, and variations between whether whole or parts are served most, occur naturally, if either is lacking, intelligence as serving the thing or organism is lacking. For as long as a whole and its parts interdepend, intelligence is involved in that interdependence, and insofar as a whole–parts organism itself is part of a larger whole and has parts that are wholes with their own parts, intelligence involves, and is involved in, many levels of interdependent beings.

PURPOSE.   Intelligence is ability to engage in purposeful activity. Purpose, we recall, involves both aim and goal. Whenever an aim and its goal exist, intelligence already exists, although when a thing which aims at its goal does not attain its goal, or end, it is to that extent unintelligent. Intelligence may be a matter of degree, for we may only partly succeed in achieving our ends. Some things that survive for a while and partly attain their ends may also perish before attaining all of the ends possible for things of their kind; they are then partly unintelligent.

Intelligence as a Category of Existence

"True existence and intelligence go together."[7]

Other Theories of Intelligence

INTERNAL ONLY. In Jainism souls seeking release from reincarnation must both check inflow of *karmas* that stick to them and also shed those already acquired. Each soul achieves its ultimate goal, *mukti*, or liberation from this world, only by its own efforts. Since no one else, whether man or god, can help him, seeking assistance from others is self-defeating. If one lacks the ability to achieve the goal by himself, he will never achieve it.

EXTERNAL ONLY. Deism depicts God as a watchmaker and the world as a watch. Men play their parts according to the natures given them by God, and may do so better by observing the laws of nature which God has installed in the world. God, whose intelligence designed and created the world, is now occupied elsewhere.

TWO KINDS: INTERNAL AND EXTERNAL. George Berkeley conceived existences as of two kinds, both mental: God, the infinite Mind, and persons with finite minds. Each person has his own will, or intelligence, to perceive objects as he pleases. But God also has the power, or intelligence, to produce in human minds those ideas which he wills and which we perceive as "real things." In our experiences exist two kinds of ideas, those which we produce at will and those produced in us by God's will. So such ideas exist as a result of two kinds of intelligence, ours and God's.

ABILITY TO ADAPT TO THE NEW. John Dewey conceived man as continually struggling to survive by solving new problems as they arise. Although he recognized that old problems recur and that habits developed by solving such problems in the first place do aid in surviving, he held that intelligence is what we use to discover, explore, and solve new problems.

ABILITY TO ADAPT TO THE OLD. Many conservative cultures admonish as traditional wisdom: "Follow the tradition." This view is exemplified in Christian orthodoxy when it advocates that one should surrender his will completely to the will of God. God, as both omniscient and benevolent, both knows and wants what is best for you and knows (i.e., has the intelligence to do) what is best for you. By wisely recognizing the inferiority of human intelligence and the superiority of divine intelligence, one wisely surrenders his own will, "mind, heart, and soul, to The Lord."

No INTELLIGENCE. Both (a) materialists, or mechanists, who view all things operating mechanically, and (b) Theravada Buddhists, who view ultimate reality as *bhavanga*, an undisturbed flow of pure being, see no need for intelligence. For the latter, the only intelligence needed, so to speak, is that of eliminating ideas of intelligence along with all other ideas.

18 / PROCESS

A *process* is a continuing series of changes. My Webster's dictionary reports "process" as "a series of actions or operations conducing to an end," "a natural phenomenon marked by gradual changes that lead to a particular result," and "something going on," "advance, progress." By "process" we mean something more complicated than what has been referred to by the foregoing proposed categories, even though they are also naturally involved in complications. For a series involves two or more things or events (some would say three or more) as a minimum.

Process and Other Categories

Perhaps the best way to explore the nature of process is to review all the categories proposed thus far and to show what happens when two or more things or events embodying those categories occur in succession.

THINGS. A process involves not only two or more things or events but also is itself a thing or event. Without two or more things so related that at least one is followed by the other in succession, no process exists. But also in whatever sense the process is one process, or a whole of some sort, we can call it a thing or event.

Not only does process involve things, but things (that is, existing things) involve process. For to exist is to be temporal and to continue through time and whatever changes constitute time. So, according to the proposed hypothesis, to be a thing, anything, is to be involved in process.

DIFFERENCE. A process continues from its beginning to its end and remains the same in whatever way it so continues. But also each of the things or events is a different thing or event. Without two or more changes, each of which is different from the other, and some continuity to the series that makes it the same from beginning to end, process does not exist.

Of course, every process is both different from every other process in being a different process and the same as every other process in being a process.

CHANGE. Not only does a process involve two or more changes in succession; it involves itself also in being something that changes by going from one change to the next change in the series. Not only does a process involve a continuous series of changes; it is thereby also something permanent, because it remains the same series continuously from beginning to end.

Process involves change, but does every change involve process? If to change is to become different, and if such becoming different involves both a *before* the becoming and an *after* the becoming in which the two are successive, such a change escapes being a process only if what is before the becoming and what is after the becoming are simple (i.e., do not themselves involve changes). If they are interdependent parts of larger wholes or are interdependent with parts of their own, surely they are involved in processes. At least, if by change we mean both the coming into being of a difference, its remaining for a while, and then its going out of being, such a change is a process.

Process involves permanence, but does every permanence involve process? To be permanent is to remain the same through change, and what remains the same through two or more changes is processual. So, according to the viewpoint presented here, to be permanent is to be processual. For example, whatever is permanent continues to remain the same through all of the successive changes in the temporal processes occurring while it endures.

Substance. Not only may each of the things or events constituting a series be substantial; the process itself may be substantial. The longer it endures, or the more changes that occur within it, the more substantial it is. Although a process depends for its nature on the changes that occur within it, it may be observed to function as sluggish or rapid, as sustaining or greatly transforming, as simple or intricate, or as isolated or interactive with other processes. These functions may be thought of as properties of the process, so that it may, for example, be a long, slow, simple, isolated process.

Of course, each substance itself is something of a process, for, in whatever way it remains through time and is involved in a continuous series of changing times, it is processual.

Wholes. Although each thing or event participating in the series constituting the process is itself a whole of parts, each process, as something that continues to be the same from beginning to end, is also a whole. It is a whole of which each of the changes, and changes from one change to the next, are parts. Unless the process happens somehow to be the universe itself, it too exists as part of larger processes which are wholes in their own way.

Every existing whole, whether atom, cell, person, or earth, is also a process in the sense that it continues to exist through changing, both internally and externally, including temporally. Also, every existing part in every whole–part organization continues to exist through whatever series of changes its whole exists through and its own parts exist through.

Time. Time is processual, for time exists only when two or more events (becomings different) occur successively while something else endures (remains the same). We are saying here that existence is both temporal and processual and that both time and process are alike in consisting of successive changes in existence while such existence continues to endure. Time involves both events and duration, and process involves both changes and their continuing succession. So time is processual, and process is temporal.

SPACE. Although ideas of process and space abstracted from existence as experienced may not seem to involve each other, existing processes and spaces do involve each other because, according to the hypothesis proposed here, both are aspects of existence rather than independent kinds of being.

Process is spatial, for unless the process exists in isolation from everything else, it coexists with other things and processes. Such coexistence involves space, for space is what is between two or more things or events existing at the same time. And unless the process is utterly simple, consisting of one change (having no parts) followed by one or more other such changes, its coexisting parts are spatially related. Since, according to the present hypothesis, no process exists in isolation and no process is utterly simple, all processes involve both external and internal space.

Space involves process, because space, as what is between coexisting things or events when nothing else is between, involves time. And existing time, consisting of events and durations of varying lengths, involves simultaneities of different lengths. For example, twenty-eight successive days coexist with one month because the earth with its spatial magnitude rotates once every day, and the moon with its spatial magnitude and its spatial relations with the earth rotates around the earth once every twenty-eight days. Space is processual, because both the things within which space exists and the things existing in space are processual.

RELATIONS. Process is relational, and according to the view expressed here, relations have both external and internal aspects. Process involves external relations because each change, event, or thing in a succession is different from, other than, and thus external to, the others. Process involves internal relatedness not only in the sense that each of the changes, events, or things in the continuing succession has its own internal nature but also in the sense that all are alike in being parts of the same process.

Do existing relations always involve process? If existence involves process, then existing relations are involved in such process. But let us consider, first, ways in which relations exist in a most static kind of existence. Suppose one thing above another remained undisturbed in a geologic layer for a million years. How can the external relation between these two things be in process? And suppose that one of these things has two parts that remain undisturbed for a million years. How can such an internal relation be in process? Both such relations are in process, because the things did not become extinct but proceeded through time, a million years of time. By remaining the same through a million annual changes, multiplied by 365 daily changes, and by the molecular, atomic, and subatomic changes every day, both such static relations were able to remain static only by existing through billions of other changes with which they are interrelated and on which they were dependent.

Let us consider, next, how relations that exist in the most instantaneous way are processual. Two simultaneous events, even two having the shortest changes possible, have both their differences in being two (external relatedness) and their sameness in being both events and events existing at the same time (internal relatedness) involved in their coming into being, lasting for an instant, and going out of being, thereby embodying a series of stages in a process.

UNIVERSALS. Process involves both universals and particulars. Each change or event in a process is a particular. Each stage in a process is a particular. All are alike in being changes or stages in that process, and such likeness constitutes a universal. Of course, each process itself is a particular process and is like all other processes in being a process.

Do all existing universals and particulars involve process? If either a particular or a universal could be abstracted from, or somehow isolated in, existing, we might see them as unrelated to process. But, because it exists, each particular is involved at least in temporal process. Even the simplest, most instantaneous event involves first not being, then being, and then not being, which are three stages in a process; or, if this seems too many, first coming into being and then going out of being, which are two stages in a process.

Each universal, because existing, is involved in whatever processes its particulars are involved in. Even that universal that consists of the sameness of two simultaneous simple instantaneous events is involved in their processes. And, except for those universals that are categories of existence, each universal itself comes into being or goes out of being or both and thus has its own temporal beginning, duration, and end, and is processual in its own way.

ACTION.   Process involves both action and passion, or activity and passivity. Each event is an act, and a process is itself an action, an enaction of a series of actions. Passion, passivity, or patiency, that is, being acted on, is present in process. Being acted on involves causation (discussion of which has been reserved for part two). If what exists at one stage in a process occurs because it has been caused by what exists at a previous stage, then it is a recipient of the results of action at the previous stage and thus functions as patient relative to that stage.

Do action and passion always involve process? That action involves process should be obvious. For each act is an event which first is not, then is, and then is not, or which comes into being, endures long enough for it to occur, and then ceases to be. That being acted on also involves process should be equally obvious. For each being acted on is an event which first is not, then is, and then is not, or which comes into being, endures long enough for it to occur, and then ceases to be.

PURPOSE.   Is process always purposive? If purpose exists whenever there is change with direction such that the beginning may be said to aim at the end, or goal, and the goal may be said to be realization, actualization, or completion of the change, then it follows that every change (and thus every process) involves purpose in this very broad sense. If purpose implies plan, preconception, mental intention, then, according to the view presented here, it is doubtful whether process involves purpose.

Is purpose always processual? If all purposes are such that they first do not exist, then exist, and then do not exist, they are processual. If a purpose involves both an aim and a goal, with the aim achieving its goal, then purpose is processual. But one may ask about aims that do not achieve their goals. If they too cease to be, then process is involved.

INTELLIGENCE.   Is all process intelligent? If intelligence is ability to attain one's ends, and if every process terminates, every process is intelligent. If a process involving the attainment of many ends does not attain all of the ends which it could attain, it is less intelligent than if it adapted in ways that enabled achievement of all of its ends.

Is all process unintelligent? If each thing, including each process, is interdependent with other things, it has more to it than can be realized by itself alone. By depending on other things for the accomplishment of some of its ends, it may not terminate, and may even be in some sense interminable. To the extent that the ends of each thing, including each process, are not achieved by its nonterminating dependence on other things, it is unintelligent. Each thing, and process, is unintelligent because it eventually becomes less and less an end in itself and more and more a means to the ends of other things and processes.

Is intelligence processual? Any attainment of any end involves even minimally first unattainment and then attainment, and thus two successive stages in one direction. Is unintelligence processual? When an existing being has an end that it fails to attain, it still must come into being, aim at its end, and cease to be, and thus embody stages in a process.

CAUSATION.   Part two of this book, devoted to exploring the nature of causation, will develop further ideas about process. For, according to the present view, all existing causation involves process and all existing process involves causation.

DIALECTIC.   Part three of this book, devoted to exploring some aspects of dialectic, will add even more ideas about process. For, according to my view, all existing dialectic is processual and all existing process is dialectical.

Other Theories of Process

PROCESS IS ILLUSORY.   According to Advaita Vedanta, all process is unreal, appearing only in *maya*, illusion. *Nirguna Brahman*, the ultimate and only reality, is pure being unaffected by any change.

PROCESS IS EMANATION.   According to Plotinus, the many emanate from the One by successive stages, but there is nothing in the later stages except a diminution of the reality present in previous stages. That which is perfect in being and nature becomes progressively more imperfect in being and nature until both being and nature disintegrate completely in the Void. Although what is imperfect can never again become perfect, some souls may arrest this downward process, turn back toward higher levels, and through reason and intuition enjoy a beatific vision of earlier perfection.

PROCESS IS CYCLICAL.   Sankhya and Yoga philosophies depict unmanifest *prakriti* as perfectly quiescent, with tension between the *gunas*, for forceful tendencies, in equilibrium. Lured into manifestation in the presence of a *purusha* (soul), a process of devolution of cosmic, and personal, awareness, self-awareness, mind, sense organs, objects of sense, and so on occurs. By practicing yoga, a self can reverse the process and eliminate objects of sense, sense organs, mind, self-awareness, and awareness, thereby liberating the *purusha* and returning *prakriti* to its quiescent unmanifest state.

PROCESS IS CHANCE. *Tychism* is the theory that chance plays a genuine role in determining processes. Tychists may range in their views from holding that all occurrences, and thus processes, are a matter of pure chance to holding that chance is merely an occasional factor in causal processes. Some may hold it is always present as a factor, even if it is not the only factor.

PROCESS IS REVERSIBLE. Chemists and physicists working with symmetrical mathematical equations discover that, mathematically at least, implications can go either way (i.e., on each side of their equation sign). Some seem to assert that existing processes are temporally reversible, though I for one do not see how this is possible. Some processes are reversible in the sense that one can undo what has been done, as when I unlace my shoes after I have laced them, but I regard these as two different, successive processes, each going forward in time.

Many other theories of process might be cited, each involving great detail. A. N. Whitehead, John Dewey, Henri Bergson, Charles Sanders Peirce, Samuel Alexander, and Roy Wood Sellars each describes process in his own way. Douglas Browning has summarized some of these in *Philosophers in Process*,[1] and Lewis S. Ford and John Cobb edit a new journal, *Process Studies*,[2] aiming to keep its readers up to date with latest philosophical thinking on the subject.

PART TWO

CAUSATION

19 / CAUSE AND EFFECT

Several questions naturally occur to us when we inquire into the nature of cause and effect.

Same or Different?

Are cause and effect (1) different? (2) the same? or (3) both the same and different? If we answer yes to any one of these questions, then are cause and effect different, the same, or both, in only one way or in many ways? Then, in what ways?

1. Some say that cause and effect are different and thus not the same. An effect is different from its cause; otherwise there would be only one thing or event and not two: that is, the cause. A cause is different from its effect; otherwise there would be only one thing or event and not two: that is, the effect. A cause and its effect are different from each other; otherwise there would be only one thing or event and not two: that is, that which is both cause and effect. In whatever sense cause and effect are two and not merely one, cause and effect are different. "Cause and effect are not mere identities."[1] "The Nyaya-Vaisesikas hold the effect to be entirely different from the cause. The effect begins to exist only when it is produced. One of the [requirements] for the production of an effect is the antecedent non-existence of the cause."[2]

2. Some say that cause and effect are the same and thus not different. "The relation of cause and effect is one of absolute identity."[3] (Here Radhakrishnan is speaking of Vallabha's view of Brahman as both creator and destroyer of the universe which is

127

identical with Brahman.) And "Cause and effect are not different from each other."[4] In addition to those who say that cause and effect are identical, some say further that the effect is identical with its cause: "The theory that the effect really exists beforehand in the cause is one of the central features of the Sankhya system."[5] "This view is designated as 'the doctrine of pre-existent effects....'"[6] I am not acquainted with the view of anyone stating that the cause is identical with its effect such that the effect somehow has a prior being from which the cause is not interdependent, unless we include the goal of a purpose yet to be fulfilled as an effect rather than as a cause.

3. Some say that cause and effect "involve both identity and difference."[7]

Effect and cause are different in some sense; otherwise we would not distinguish them. Yet also there are several ways in which they are alike:

a. A cause and its effect are involved in a cause–effect relationship. To be a cause is to produce an effect and to be an effect is to be produced by a cause. Cause and effect are alike in sharing this same relation. This sameness may be seen more clearly if we examine some examples: "Spark causes explosion." "Rain causes flood." Even if spark and explosion are different, and rain and flood are different, both "spark and explosion" and "rain and flood" have more in common than "spark" and "flood."

b. Something in the cause is carried over into the effect. At least part of the gene structure of parents continues on in their offspring. "$E = MC^2$." Whether "matter" is transformed into "energy" or "energy" is transformed into "matter," something is presumed to remain the same or at least "equal."

c. Both cause and effect are parts of a larger whole (or even several larger wholes); at least they are parts of "the universe as a whole." In whatever sense they are the same in participating in the same larger whole, they are the same and not different.

Hence being different in some sense and the same in some sense or senses, cause and effect involve both some identity and some difference. How much sameness and how much difference are involved in all cause–effect relationships is a question that I do not feel warranted in generalizing about. Some kinds of cause–effect relations seems to involve much more difference than others, and some seem to involve much more sameness than others. There may even be increasing or decreasing difference occurring during a cause–effect process. Such generalizations are tasks for more specific sciences.

Continuous or Discontinuous?

Are cause and effect discontinuous, continuous, or both? Continuity is one kind of sameness, the sameness of something continuing through time. Some say that, since an effect is not its cause and a cause is not its effect, there must be some place where the cause stops and the effect begins. There may even be a gap of some sort between cause and effect. If the world is made up of a series of events, each one different from the others, which occur successively, then a later event may be caused by an earlier event with which it is not contiguous and thus would not be continuous. Others say that the cause "is existentially continuous with" the effect.[8] "Cause and effect are spatio-temporally continuous."[9]

My view is that cause and effect are both in some sense continuous and in some sense discontinuous. For insofar as cause and effect are different, their sameness ceases or discontinues, and insofar as cause and effect are alike, their sameness continues. Some cause–effect eventities appear to involve more continuity and some more discontinuity. Some cause–effect eventities appear to involve more continuity of some kinds and more discontinuity of other kinds. When a child is born, dependence of his life on his mother's life discontinues, but family genetic traits continue.

Related Internally or Externally?

Are cause and effect related internally or externally or both? Since we have identified internal relatedness with sameness and external relatedness with difference, it seems unnecessary to repeat here the types of views that are relevant. Whereas some say that cause and effect are externally related, and some say that they are internally related, the view presented here proposes that every relation involves both internal and external aspects and that every cause–effect relation involves both some internal and some external aspects, and that cause and effect may be related more externally than internally in some ways and more internally than externally in other ways.

Independent or Dependent?

Are cause and effect (1) independent of each other, (2) dependent on each other, or (3) interdependent?

1. If cause and effect are independent of each other, are they completely independent or partly independent? If completely independent, then they are unrelated; so there can be no cause–effect relation and no causation. If only partly independent, then they are interdependent (see treatment under 3, below).

2. If cause and effect are dependent, in what ways are they dependent?

a. Some say that cause and effect are such that the effect depends on the cause but that the cause does not depend on the effect. For example, a gun accidentally discharges and kills a man, but the death of the man did not cause the gun to discharge.

b. Some say that cause and effect are such that the cause depends on the effect but that the effect does not depend on the cause. To be a cause is to produce an effect; if no effect can be produced, there can be no cause. Therefore, the cause depends on the producibility and the actual production of an effect in order for it to be a cause. For example, my wife prepares my meals because I eat them; but if I did not eat the meals, then she would not prepare them.

c. Some say that cause and effect are such that each depends on the other completely. To be a cause is to produce an effect and to be an effect is to be produced by a cause. Without cause there can be no cause–effect relation and without effect there can be no cause–effect relation. Both are equally necessary, and neither could be what it is without the other being what it is. For example, a playground swing moving back and forth (causing nothing) suddenly hits Johnnie on the head (causing pain). The swing could not be the cause of pain until the pain was produced; the effect had to occur before the moving swing could become its cause. And the effect (pain) did not exist until produced by the cause (moving swing hitting head). Each is thus completely dependent on the other for its being what it is as cause and effect.

3. If cause and effect are interdependent (i.e., partly dependent on and partly independent of each other), how much independence and how much dependence do each have relative to the other? In the foregoing example, the moving swing existed prior to, during, and even after hitting the head. It existed independently of Johnnie's head. And Johnnie's head also existed prior to, during, and after being hit. It had existence independent of the moving swing. But the collision depended on both, or each depended on the other for the collision. Hence the causal situation involved both the independence of swing and head from each other and the dependence of swing and head on each other. There was more to Johnnie's head than its being hit by the swing, even when it was hit; and there was more to the swing than its hitting Johnnie's head, even when it hit. These "moves" involve independence in a situation in which such hitting clearly involves interdependence.

Being interdependent (i.e., partly independent of and partly dependent on each other) does not necessarily involve exactly equal independence and dependence. For some effects seem to be more dependent on than independent of their causes. Some effects seem to be more independent of than dependent on their causes. Some causes seem to be more dependent on than independent of their effects. Some causes seem more independent of than dependent on their effects. And some causes and effects seem to depend on, and be independent of, each other equally.

More or Less?

"More or less of what?" we ask. Just as there are different kinds of causation, depending on the kinds of things or processes that are involved, so there are many different kinds of "more": more power, more potentiality, more actuality, more substantiality, more novelty, more alternatives or opportunities. We shall attempt to limit our treatment here to generalizations about what all cause–effect situations have in common, including the differences from each other they have in common.

1. Some say that there is always more in the cause than in the effect. Orthodox theism, viewing God as the creator of the world, typically holds that God is more powerful, more knowing, and more good than what he creates. Some conceive this difference in terms of perfection and imperfection. Vedantists regard Brahman, and Sankhya-Yogins regard *prakriti*, as more complete or perfect in their unmanifest state than any of their manifestations. Plato and Plotinus hold that the Ideas and The One are more perfectly real than any creature patterned after or embodying the Ideas or emanating from The One. These views hold that God, Brahman, unmanifest *prakriti*, the Ideas and The One are, in any cause–effect situation, always cause and never effect.

If and when a creature ceases, either by completely ceasing to exist or by being reabsorbed somehow into the cause, such cessation or reabsorption in no way effects the perfection of the cause but is merely another effect on the effect. When creation is conceived in a monohierarchical manner, the doctrine that there is always more in the cause than in the effect can be carried out completely down to the most minute effect.

2. Some say that there is always more in the effect than in the cause.

a. At this writing, I do not recall a specific clear example, but the spirit or intent of some creation myths appears to be groping for a view something like the following. Before the beginning, there was nothing. Nothing was completely void of anything. But somehow that void existed as a lack of something. That lack of something, or want of something, served as a source of the coming into being of something. Thus from nothing came something, first one thing, then another, and then another. The solitariness, aloneness, perhaps loneliness, of the first thing existed as lack of any other thing, and this lack of another thing, like the original lack of anything, served as a source of, or cause of, a second thing. All things that come into existence thus are effects of whatever brought them into being. If the original nothing, with its lack of something, was the original cause of all somethings as effects, then there is always more in the effects than in this original cause.

b. The once-prevalent notion of spontaneous generation of things, such as germs, seems to imply causation of something from nothing and thus of more in the effect than in the cause.

c. Extreme voluntarists, romanticists, and existentialists idealize will as the ultimate reality, perhaps even the only reality, and each act of will as *sui generis*. Thus they presuppose that uncaused will produces will-caused effects. This ideal is epitomized in the view that holds that *existenz* (i.e., each uncaused act of will) is "authentic" only when it refuses to permit itself to be influenced (i.e., caused) by anything else—whether laws of society, laws of logic, laws of nature, physical things, other persons, or even one's own previous willings. Most people who hold this view admit that such "authenticity" is difficult to attain and maintain but nevertheless claim that attainment is both possible and, ideally, perpetually actualizable.

3. Some say that there is always exactly as much in the cause as in the effect and exactly as much in the effect as in the cause. "$E = MC^2$." The total amount of matter and/or energy constituting the universe is fixed, and matter and/or energy can be neither created nor destroyed. So, in any cause–effect situation, energy may be transformed into matter or matter may be transformed into energy, but the total amount of matter and/or energy is neither created nor diminished thereby. This theory has a corollary stated as "for every action there is an equal and opposite reaction." Some pantheists hold a similar view: that God is everything and everything is or is within God. Hence every cause and every effect, being within or part of God, involve God as both cause of every effect and effect of every cause.

4. Some say that there is sometimes more in the cause than in the effect, sometimes more in the effect than in the cause, and sometimes equally as much in the cause as in the effect. Although these may be superficial observations, everyday experience provides plenty of examples of these differences. Some couples produce ten children, some produce one child or no children, and some have two children, thus exactly reproducing themselves numerically. Sometimes the swing of a hammer causes a landslide; sometimes we pound and pound and pound, and the thing pounded refuses to budge; sometimes we swing one hammer against another that bounces away with equal force. Some people seem to receive less than they deserve; some seem to receive more than they deserve; and some seem to get what they deserve; we observe these same injustices and justices relative to our own efforts.

This view has been stated more precisely by emergentists such as C. Lloyd Morgan (in his *Emergent Evolution*).[10] He distinguishes between "resultants" (i.e., cause–effect situations in which effects are always exactly equal to their causes) and "emergents" (i.e., situations involving the emergence of novelty, or new levels of being, with new things that have new substantiality, new functions, new capacities, new causal efficacy, and thus more in the effect than in their causes). Emergentists also admit the destruction, cessation, or demergence of emergents so that, as a consequence, there is less in such results than in their causes.[11]

5. Some say that there is always both more of something in the cause than in the effect, more of something else in the effect than in the cause, and also some equality between cause and effect.

Traditional theists, Vedantists, and others, who hold that there is always more in the cause than in the effect, mean not only that there is more unity, permanence, substance, or goodness in the cause but also that there is more plurality, impermanence, or evil in the effect. If the cause is, or has, more in the sense of being more perfect than the effect, then the effect, necessarily, is more imperfect or has more of whatever that which is imperfect has. Although it may be less clear how perfect cause and imperfect effect can be equal, they are equally opposed to each other. These views usually incorporate notions of justice, *karma*, or the Days and Nights of Brahman, which tend to mitigate the seeming injustice involved in having two unequal kinds of beings.

I subscribe to this view, which will be more fully explicated below. Here I merely assert the claim that in every cause–effect situation there is always (a) something more in the cause (which ceases when the cause ceased to exist) than in the effect; (b) something more in the effect (which comes into being only when the effect comes into being); and (c) some equality of cause and effect, such that each effect perpetuates something in its cause and each cause is somewhat perpetuated in its effects. Thus somehow the universe as a whole in the long run gains about as much as it loses and loses about as much as it gains through all its cause–effect processes. Although I regard as sheer speculation any decision choosing between theories of the expanding universe, the contracting universe, and the pulsating universe, I happen to prefer the last.

6. Some say that there are two or three different kinds of causation: those in which there is more in the cause than in the effect, those in which there is more in the effect than in the cause, and those in which cause and effect are equal. Without repeating the evidence cited in 4 above, we here focus on the tendency of some to divide different kinds of things into mutually exclusive classes. Descartes-like dualists hold that there are two kinds of being, matter and spirit. Material things always conform to the principle of the conservation of matter; matter can be neither created nor destroyed, and thus there can never be any more or any less matter as a result of any cause–effect process. But spirit, which has free will, can cause effects that it wills without in any way diminishing its will and its power to will. Descartes himself supplemented his spirit–matter dualism with a third kind of causation: God who, though perfect, created a world that is imperfect and thus has in it as effect less than its cause.

7. Finally, and yet without exhausting all of the possibilities, we include the view of those who say that every distinction between cause and effect is illusory. Ultimate reality, both *Nirguna Brahman* of Shankara and *sunya* of Nagarjuna, is devoid of distinctions between cause and effect. Any apparent cause–effect distinctions are unreal.

One or Many?

Are cause and effect such that (1) each cause has only one effect and each effect is the effect of only one cause; (2) each cause produces many effects; (3) each effect is the product of many causes; (4) every cause has many effects and every effect is a product of many causes; or (5) different causes and effects differ with respect to whether there are one or many causes and one or many effects?

For purposes of simplification, we often speak of a cause and an effect as if there were only one of each. "The Nyaya believes that there is no plurality and there is only one cause for one effect."[12] Most theorists seem to hold that most, if not all, effects have many causes and most, if not all, causes have many effects. Exceptions to those views hold that one god or creator is one cause of all of the many creatures.

These questions become more complicated when we inquire: (1) whether the many effects are all simultaneous, all successive, or both, and whether the many causes are all simultaneous, all antecedently successive, or both; (2) whether the causes are all of one kind (e.g., material or spiritual, or efficient or final) or of two or more kinds, and whether the effects are all of one kind or of two or more kinds, and what happens when these kinds interact (i.e., do they produce new kinds of effects, both kinds of effects, or no kinds of effects); and (3) whether the causes are all of one level or of different levels (see treatment of levels of causation, below).

20 / CAUSE AND CHANGE

To change is to become different, and to become different is to change. To cause is to produce an effect, and to be an effect is to be produced by a cause. Four questions naturally arise when we become aware of these statements: (1) Does every change require a cause? Or can there be change without cause? (2) Does every cause require a change? Or can there be causation without change? (3) What about permanence? Does every remaining the same require a cause? Or can there be permanence, or remaining the same, without cause? (4) What about effects? Does every effect require a change? Or can there be effects that are not effects of change?

The view that there can be no change without cause seems to be a matter of common sense until we explore the issue more deeply. Cause–effect situations usually seem such that there can be no effect without something becoming different. In examining views about whether cause and effect are the same or different, we noted that some hold that an effect must be partly different from its cause, and others that an effect must be completely different. These views assert, or imply, that there can be no cause that does not cause a change and that there can be no effect that does not require a change. But there are also views that hold that cause and effect are not different and thus do not involve change. Only that which remains the same, timelessly or eternally, is real. Thus all change is illusory, and any appearance of cause and effect involving change is also illusory.

When we stop to think about it, we realize that our buildings can continue to exist only if their foundations continue to remain the same. Their remaining the same (i.e., substantial or permanent) is necessary for their continuance. Hence, such substantiality, such remaining the same, is a cause of the building's continuing. Permanence of the building depends on, or is caused by, the unchangingness or permanence of its foundation. So, also, the permanence of the building is an effect of no change or of unchangingness. If this is so, then not every effect requires a change and not every cause produces a change.

However, in the foregoing we have ignored change in time as a kind of change. If a building remains the same through time, it can do so only through remaining the same at different (i.e., changing) times. If there can be no cause and effect without change in time, then there can be no cause and no effect without change, because in this sense there can be no permanence without change.

But does every change require a cause? We cannot deduce an answer from the foregoing evidence. We need a further hypothesis: that nothing happens without a cause. From this hypothesis it would follow that there can be neither change nor permanence without a cause. The view presented here proposes this additional hypothesis and regards both cause and effect and change and permanence as categories (i.e., universal characteristics) of existence. Such a hypothesis remains to be demonstrated. It involves the implication that every change involves a cause and that every cause involves a change, and also that every permanence involves a cause and that every cause involves some permanence. No cause terminates completely in any one of its effects.

21 / CAUSE AND OTHER CONDITIONS

One of Aristotle's most famous theories postulates "four causes" of the existence of each thing. Aristotle called these the material, formal, final, and efficient causes. The material cause is the stuff of which a thing is made, as when a table is made of wood. The formal cause is the form that the thing takes when it comes into being, as when pieces of wood are placed together in the form of a table. The final cause is the purpose for which a thing comes into existence, as when the desire of a person to have something convenient on which to eat or write motivates him to make the table. The efficient cause is the power or effort involved in the act of bringing a thing into being, as when a carpenter manufactures a table. Only the last of these four, the efficient cause, is that which produces effects. On the other hand, if all four are required for the existence of every thing, then are they not all causes of the existence of that thing?[1]

We have come to make a distinction between cause (i.e., efficient causation) and condition (sometimes referred to as "necessary and sufficient condition"). If there are some conditions without which a thing cannot exist, are not all of them causal, or parts of the total cause, of the existence of that thing? If so, then inquiry into the nature of causality is incomplete until all necessary and sufficient conditions are understood. Are there only the four that Aristotle proposed? Or are there more? If by "category of existence" we mean a universal characteristic or condition of existence, then are not all of such categories conditions for its existence; and hence are not all of them causes in this sense? There is a sense in which the entire metaphysical enterprise (i.e., inquiry into the existence and its categories) is an inquiry into the nature of causation. Our treatment of causality will be incomplete until we show how all other categories of existence are related to it as essential conditions.

To summarize, the question is raised: Is efficient causation, which consists of a cause producing an effect, only one of the kinds of conditions, and thus only one of several kinds of the causes, of existence of each thing? This question should help to dispel any notion that causation is simple. It may be that every effect is a product of a complex gestalt or creative synthesis of a multiplicity of conditions as well as of efficient causes. Perhaps there is nothing more complex than causation. We hope to explore at least some of these complicated factors below.

22 / CAUSE AND DIRECTION

A seemingly minor problem involved in understanding causality has to do with whether the cause–effect relation is directional. The usual view is that direction is involved and that it is always from cause to effect, never from effect to cause. "A cause brings its effect into existence, but an effect does not bring its cause into existence. . . ."[1] Such a view involves a "priority of time in the cause before the effect."[2] Three kinds of questions have arisen on this view.

Cause and Effect as Reversible

Attempts to interpret causal situations mathematically have led to the view that the direction from cause to effect is reversible. "$E = MC^2$." The equation, $=$, implies that $C = E$, that cause equals effect. But equality, $=$, is a symmetrical relation. If A is equal to B, then B is equal to A. If C is equal to E, then E is equal to C. When C and E are represented by numbers, there is nothing in the equation that requires one to precede the other. Some who seem to have become preoccupied with, or enamored of, mathematical equations appear to have concluded that the direction may be from effect to cause just as well as from cause to effect or, if they regard equality as essentially two-directional, that both effect–cause and cause–effect directions are always present in causation.

Effect as Influence on Cause

Purpose is sometimes interpreted as involving not merely a goal that will be reached eventually at some future time, but a goal that has a drawing power, something like a magnet, which pulls developing things toward it. Disputes have arisen over whether the pull or the push is stronger in bringing some kinds of things into being or to their fulfillment. "There is nothing so powerful as an idea whose time has come." A person's life is guided by the ideals he keeps or which keep him under their control. Their lack of fulfillment causes us to work to fulfill them. If the effect, as yet unactualized, lures us toward it, does it function causally? If so, is the direction of power from effect to cause? Or if we admit that the unfulfilled effect actually causes fulfillment, does what is future, the yet-to-be-fulfilled effect, cause what is present (i.e., our present efforts toward fulfilling it)?

Cause and Effect as Simultaneous

The view that cause–effect relations are always directional (i.e., from cause to effect) is challenged by another question: Are cause and effect ever contemporary? Although fuller exploration of this challenge must await the following treatment of cause and time, we mention three forms of this challenge.

1. Some claim that cause and effect partially overlap. Unless cause must cease to exist before effect can begin to exist, there must be at least some point where they exist together. If so, then how can there be direction in time for things which are simultaneous? Before they are simultaneous, we can say the cause is directed toward the effect, and after they are simultaneous, we can say that the effect comes from the direction of the cause. But while they are simultaneous, can there be any direction?

2. Some claim that cause and effect are completely contemporary. Two such views may be cited. Those who say the universe exists only in the present and the present exists for only an infinitesimal instant, must hold (a) that all actual causation occurs within such infinitesimal instant and (b) that such instant is too short for cause and effect to be differentiated. Hence, any cause–effect situation that exists must exist for so short a time that no direction is possible. Those who say that the universe (*Nirguna Brahman*) is nontemporal and that distinctions between both cause and effect and past, present, and future are illusory, and thus that cause and effect are, in reality, nondifferent or identical, must hold that no actual cause–effect direction exists.

Hume condemned the view that "any cause may be perfectly contemporary with its effect" by saying that, if it were, then "this effect with its effect, and so on, it is plain that there would be no such thing as succession, and all objects must be co-existent."[3]

3. Some say that two mutually sustaining things function both as cause and as effect of each other's maintenance. When this is the case, each of the two things is both cause and effect simultaneously. Direction is simultaneously as much from one to the other as from the other to the one. Such causation may be illustrated by the two sides of an arch, each of which causes the other to remain in its position. It may be illustrated also by whole–part causation: The nature and perpetuation of a whole of parts depend, causally, on its parts and its parts depend, causally, on it as a whole. (See the discussions below on whole–part causation and levels of causation.)

Cause and Effect as Interrelated

My tentative conclusions about cause and direction are that, although there can be no causation without time (see following chapter) and no time without direction, and thus no causation without some succession in which cause precedes effect, there can be, and probably always is, both some simultaneity of cause and effect in every cause–effect situation and some influence upon the cause by the effect which involves some effect–cause direction also. How all this can be and is so will be explained more fully, in the discussion of whole–part causation and levels of causation.

23 / CAUSE AND TIME

Two of the most complex problems in metaphysics deal with understanding causation and time. When we consider their interrelations, additional questions may provoke our thinking.

Can There Be Causation without Time?

Some say no. Sellars claims that "Causality is a temporal affair in the relations of things. It involves changes in existence."[1] Others say yes. Orthodox Christian theologians have claimed (1) that God, in creating the world, created or caused time, which act of creation was not in time or temporal; (2) that God as an eternal, timeless, or nontemporal being is *essentially* a creator, hence *eternally* a creator; (3) that being a creator essentially, eternally, entails creation (i.e., causation); and (4) that such creation and causation subsisted eternally prior to time and hence without the existence of time. This claim, entailing the paradoxical view that creation, aimed at perfection, involves a completely perfect being in causing imperfection for the purpose of demonstrating capacity to produce some perfection. This view also implies that the causation of time was a timeless act, both just prior to the actualization of time and eternally.

Both yes and no answers to the questions of causation without time challenge further thinking.

I favor the view that there can be no causation without time, but for somewhat different reasons than those Sellars gives. Two reasons can be given here.

1. Time involves both events and duration, both becoming dif-

ferent and remaining the same, both change and permanence. Causation is a temporal affair not merely because it involves changes but also because it involves permanences or, rather, because both change and permanence are involved in every cause–effect situation. Both changes and permanences, both events and durations, both becoming different and remaining the same, are caused. And changes cause and permanences cause, so to speak, in the sense that effects in becoming different are caused by changes and effects in remaining the same are caused by permanences. In every cause–effect situation, the effect involves some temporal difference from the cause and some temporal sameness with the cause, some succession and some simultaneity. To the extent that duration (i.e., remaining the same without change) is an aspect of time which can be interpreted as an eternity, all time (and hence all causation) involves such a timeless aspect. This may seem to be a trivial aspect; yet it provides some basis for extrapolating speculations about causation without time.

2. My tentative commitment to the hypothesis that both time and causation are categories (i.e., universal characteristics) of existence commits me further, by implication, to the view that there can be no causation without time and no time without causation, because no universal characteristics can exist without the presence of all other universal characteristics of existence.

How Are Cause and Time Interrelated?

If cause and time interdepend such that there can be neither causation without time nor time without causation, and if time is complex, then causation is also complex. Some of the ways in which causation is complex, relative to time, may be summarized by reviewing complexities involved in our multiple-aspect theory of time. Past, present, and future will be treated here. Others will be treated in later sections.

PRESENT.   Consider three kinds of questions relative to causation and the present: those pertaining to (1) causation in the present, (2) causation of the present, and (3) causation by the present.

1. *Is all causation in the present?* Some say that only the present exists. The past no longer exists. The future does not yet exist. Since only the present exists, all existing causation must be in the present. If causation involves both cause and effect, then all causes are present, all effects are present, and all of both causes and effects are present. Such a view seems to imply that what is past does not cause what is present and what is present does not cause what is future, or that what is present cannot be an effect of what is past and what will be future cannot be an effect of what is present. Thus all causation except present self-causation seems to be eliminated.

2. *Is what is present caused by what is past?* Some say that only what is past can be the cause of what is present. What is present is an effect which has been caused. Cause precedes effect. Therefore cause, which precedes its present effects, must be past. What is present must be caused by what is past; otherwise the present would be self-causing, or self-existing, and would not need to be caused by anything other than itself. But such a view seems to imply elimination of all possibility of causation during the present.

3. *Can what is present cause what is future?* Some ask, if only the present exists and no future exists, how can that which exists cause that which does not exist? If what is present were now a cause, it would have to be the cause of a nonexistent future effect. But if and when a future effect exists, what is now present must have become past and have ceased to exist. Hence, what is present cannot *be* the cause of what is future but can only *have been* the cause of what *was to have been* in its future. What is present cannot, as present, be the cause of what is future, but only as past (i.e., after it becomes past) can it be (i.e., have been) the cause of what has become present. Such a view implies that what is

present cannot be the cause of what is future but only of what exists at another present.

These three views are too simple-minded, because they presuppose that what is present is sharply divided from what is past and what is future by excluded middles. Although there is a fundamental sense in which it is true that only what is present exists, it is also true, as we have shown elsewhere (see the chapter on time, above), that there is no single present but that there are many presents, one for each event or eventity that requires its own time to occur or endure. Some events take longer to occur and some durations endure longer than others. Thus some presents are longer than others, and what is present relative to one event may be partly past, or partly future, or partly both, relative to another. Even if causation were limited to what is present, one cause might continue to produce its effect while another cause which started to produce its effect at the same time may have finished its effect and ceased to be as a cause before the first cause finished being a cause.

Consider a series of events such as getting out of bed, cleaning my teeth, shaving, dressing, eating breakfast, and departing for work, all in a single morning. When I start to shave, after lathering my face, I take one stroke of my razor, then another, then another, and so on, until all whiskers seem removed. Each stroke of my razor is an event that begins and ends and lasts from beginning to end. While it is occurring, it is a present stroke. Each successive stroke, whether longer or shorter, also exists as a present stroke. But the event of my shaving, which also began and ended and lasted from beginning to end, is an event, and a present event, with its own present duration. And the whole process of shaving is a part of my behavior on a single morning, which began when I arose and ended when I departed for work and lasted from beginning to end, and functioned as a present time, in contrast with my just-past sleep and my just-future work. Of course, the shaving and other events are all part of a larger whole of my life, that is, of earning a living and of maintaining my health, security, friendship, and happiness. In a sense, all of these participated causally in my shaving. And my shaving participated causally in producing or supporting them.

This example reveals causation to be not merely complicated, but complicated in ways in which particular events, such as razor strokes, interdepend with larger events and processes such as making a living and as living a life. Involved are causation of parts by wholes and wholes by parts and several levels of causation, which we have yet to discuss. Seeing causation as involving levels of time and levels of whole-part interdependencies of events each existing with presents of different lengths, we can recognize that existence is such that every way in which cause exists in the present is supplemented by ways in which causes and effects exist also as past and as future relative to it.

In response to the three questions relating to causation and the present, I answer that there is a sense in which all causation is present, there is a sense in which what is present is caused by what is past, and there is a sense in which what is present causes what is future, and that these different senses not only are compatible with each other but that each refers to an aspect of every cause–effect situation. That is, every cause–effect situation is complex and multiaspected, and a person does not fully understand the nature of causation until he becomes aware of all of such many aspects. More of them will be explored below.

PAST. In addition to previous questions involving the past, we here inquire, not "Did what is past cause what is present?" but "Does what is past cause what is present?" or "Is what is past still causing what is present?" or "Is what is present still being caused by what is past?"

1. First, let us consider *the immediate past.* If what is present is what it is because it was caused by what is past, do not the effects of that cause continue to exist? If the causes of what is present had been different, then what is present would be differ-

ent. If whatever difference now exists does exist because it was caused, to what extent does the cause continue to function in the present? Does any functioning of a past cause in the present constitute a continuing of that cause in that functioning? We have discussed previously whether and to what extent cause and effect are the same as well as different, continuous as well as discontinuous, and overlapping as well as exclusive. To the extent that an effect is the same as its cause, to the extent that an effect is continuous with its cause, and to the extent that an effect overlaps its cause, we may say that what is present is still being caused by a cause that is also partly past. We have also discussed (and will discuss further below) how part–whole and whole–part causation involves continuing causation of successive parts by continuingly simultaneous wholes. Here the issue of levels of time and levels of causation reveals how what is present in one way is caused by what is past in another way.

We may observe that different kinds of causes produce different kinds of effects and do so in different ways. How many kinds of causes, and in how many ways may causes, produce effects? We answer, as many as there are kinds of things caused and as many as there are ways in which things are caused. It does not matter whether the effect is like or different from the cause. The effect still is what it is, whether as like or as different from, its cause, and this likeness or difference continues to constitute it as present. It continues to be caused by all the conditions that sustain it, and those conditions continue to function in it now.

This issue is often discussed in terms of delimitation, determination, and even, in personified ways, decision. "We mean by causation the delimitation of the future by the present and the past."[2] Causation, as we shall see below, involves creation in the sense that what follows is in some sense new and different from what existed before. Each causal act in which alternative and mutually exclusive possibilities are decided in terms of one versus the other determines not only the present but the whole course of the future. We refer to this characteristic of causation when we say, "As the twig is bent so the tree will grow," "I am a part of all that I have met," "Cultural heritage determines attitudes."

2. Next, consider *the remote past*. If what is present is still being caused by what is past, how long past can something have been and still be causing what is present? If determinants of the sort discussed in the previous chapter decide courses of action permanently, do all past events that causally determine the course of events after them continue to have effects in the present? The complexity of such ideas staggers the imagination that seeks an easier mode of apprehension. For if every cause somehow has its own, no matter how little, effect on every succeeding event, then does each cause produce effects perpetually and infinitely? If so, then every effect is an effect of a multiplicity of causes, and perhaps an infinity of previous causes.

On the other hand, if each cause has to share with all other causes, contemporary and successive, in producing each event as effect, it may be that the relative amount of effectiveness it has diminishes as processes continue and that diminution eventually becomes insignificant if not nonexistent. Regardless of whether a cause ever does or does not cease to be effective in some minimal way, at least here is an aspect of causation that needs to be taken into consideration in any fully adequate account of it.

Some minds, confused by such intricacy, propose the hypothesis of a "first cause," or an uncaused cause, to stop the infinity; and some propose an end to time and to causation to stop future infinity. But these proposals have their own difficulties. Some of these will be considered below. (See "Uncaused Causation," chapter 27.)

FUTURE. Regarding causation and the future, two main kinds of questions occur. Does what is present cause what is future? Does what is future cause what is present?

1. Disregarding questions related to views that the future does not exist and so cannot be caused by what is present, we consider

only the following alternatives. Some say that what is present will cause what will be in the future. Some ask if what is present is now causing what will be future. That is, do present decisions determine what will be in the future? Some ask if what is present now is causing what is future. The last question implies that what is future is somehow already involved in what is present. If, as previously noted, cause and effect are both same and different, continuous and discontinuous, and partly overlapping and partly nonoverlapping, is not that which is future already being shaped in whatever sense what is future is the same as what is present; in whatever sense what is future is continuous with what is present; and in whatever sense what is future overlaps what is present? In whatever sense what is future is part of a larger whole that is present as a whole during a series of successive parts each having its own present, what is present during each such part contributes to, or causes, the whole which is partly future relative to it; and indirectly, through its influence upon that whole, it contributes to or causes parts which, though future relative to it, are already being brought into existence by the whole of which they will be parts. (See chapter 24, "Whole–Part Causation.")

2. More interesting, and more controversial, is the question: Does what is future cause what is present? Some are quick to say, "Of course not! Causation is directional: Cause always precedes effect." Others point to the pull of ideals, of goals, on human behavior. The evidence seems sufficient for some to speak of a final cause, the end of a process, as a cause, perhaps the most important cause, of the existence and nature of things. But disputes continue over whether this holds for all things or only some things and whether values are involved in some or all causation. (See chapter 29, "Final Causation.")

A third view appeals to whole–part causation, to be discussed further in the following chapter. Whenever a present part of a whole is caused, not merely by temporally antecedent parts, but also by the nature of the whole (which cannot be the whole that it is without all its parts, including those which will succeed our present part), do these parts, which are future relative to it but somehow essential to constituting the temporal whole of which it is part, have some influence on it through their influence upon the whole? If we grant truth to this view, then we must ask, if there are many levels of whole–part relations, is each part influenced by all the higher-level and longer-lasting wholes? Some say yes. But others, perhaps trying to avoid mind boggling, postulate a single largest whole, the universe, which puts an end to higher-level influences by a larger whole.

If we grant the foregoing, then we can inquire if not only the present, but also what is past, relative to any present, is still being caused by what is future. As a part of the same question, is what is present now having some cause on what is past? Such a line of questioning can lead us further to inquire whether there is some circular process of causation whereby what is past causes what is future and what is future causes what is past, which what is past causes that same what is future. If what is past and what is future interdepend, and interact, in any way, may there be reciprocating influences, even rhythmically reciprocating influences between what is past and what is future? We can hardly resolve these questions until we more fully comprehend whole–part causation and levels of causation.

24 / WHOLE-PART CAUSATION

Probably there is no more important, and at the same time no more neglected, aspect of causation than the mutual causation, or intercausation, of wholes and parts.

Reasons for the neglect are easy to find. First, such causation is relatively difficult to comprehend both because it is intricately complex in nature and because it involves aspects that do not lend themselves to what has traditionally been called clear thinking. The second reason flows from the first: We have developed philosophies that idealize clarity and distinctness, both in conception and measurement, and that tend to ignore, and even deny the existence of, what does not lend itself to such ideals.

Prevalent philosophies which presuppose that existence is inherently rational, logical, and mathematically measurable ("If it can't be measured, it doesn't exist") tend naturally and necessarily to deny that existence, including existing causation, is such that it cannot be understood completely by such methods. Those views tend to presuppose atomic (indivisible) events, atomic facts, and atomic elements of propositions and a doctrine of external relations in both existence and logic. However, if we are to understand fully the nature of causation, we need both an organic (i.e., whole–part) metaphysics and an organic logic. We do not have time to develop such a logic here, except as implicit in our treatment of whole–part causation. (See previous chapters on wholes and parts, relations, and the following chapter on levels of causation.)

Recall that by "whole" we mean "a whole of parts" and by "part" we mean "a part of a whole." Such a meaning precludes thinking of a whole without parts or a part without a whole. A whole and its parts interdepend. That is, on the one hand, each depends on the other for supplying something essential to its nature. A part cannot be a part of a whole unless there is such a whole for it to be a part of. A whole cannot be a whole of parts unless there are such parts for it to be a whole of. Furthermore, each part depends on all the other parts for their contributions to the whole as something dependent on them.

On the other hand, the whole and every part has some being of its own that exists to be depended on. There is something more to each part than its being a part of the whole, and there is something more to the whole than its functioning as a whole in relation to each part and to all of its parts. That is, to say that whole and parts interdepend is to say that whole and parts are partly dependent on each other and partly independent of each other.

In some whole–part relations, the wholes and parts are more independent of than dependent on each other. In others, they are more dependent on than independent of each other. Sometimes a whole is more dependent on its parts than its parts are on it; sometimes a part is more dependent on its whole than its whole on it. Such variations in degrees (and different parts too may depend differentially on the whole and on other parts) complicate the nature of whole–part causation.

Relations of Causation with Wholes and Parts

Inquiring about the interrelations of cause and effect and of wholes and parts, we face a series of questions.

1. a. Is each cause a whole? Is there a whole of each cause? b. Is each effect a whole? Is there a whole of each effect? c. Is each cause–effect situation a whole: Is there a whole of each cause–effect situation?

2. a. Is each cause a part? That is, is each cause a part of some

whole of causation, or of a whole that also has other characteristics, including categories? b. Is each effect a part? That is, is each effect a part of some whole of effects, or of a whole that has other characteristics? c. Is each cause–effect situation a part? That is, does each cause–effect situation participate in some larger cause–effect situations?

3. a. Is each whole a cause? b. Is each part a cause? c. Is each whole–parts existent (i.e., each organic whole, meaning that which is the whole of both the whole and its parts) a cause?

4. a. Is each whole an effect? That is, is each whole caused? b. Is each part an effect? That is, is each part caused? c. Is each whole–part (i.e., organic whole) an effect? That is, is it caused?

Although others may disagree, I see no reason for not saying yes to each of the foregoing questions. Likewise I see a need for recognizing additional kinds or aspects of causation relative to each organic whole. Some of these may be summarized as follows.

Whenever a whole–part situation exists: 1. Is there causation of the whole by the parts?

2. Is there causation of each part by the whole?

3. Is there causation of the parts by each other? Do parts causally influence each other in at least three ways: a. Do parts influence each other directly (i.e., when one part influences a part next to it)? b. Do parts influence each other indirectly (i.e., when one part causes another to influence still another, etc.)? c. Do parts influence each other through influencing the whole which in turn influences some or all the parts as a consequence?

4. Does the whole influence the parts more than the parts influence the whole? This question remains ambiguous until we ask: a. Does the whole influence each part more than each part influences the whole? b. Does the whole influence all the parts together more than all of the parts together influence the whole? To these questions some will say yes, the whole is more influential. Some will say no, the parts are more influential. Some will say no, because whole and parts are equally influential. Some will say no,

for sometimes the whole influences the parts more than the parts influence the whole and sometimes the parts influence the whole more than the whole influences the parts. And some will say this about some kinds of whole–part situations, while others will say that this is true of all whole–part situations. My view is that there are, indeed, variations, of both kinds and degrees. I also believe that there is a sense in which a whole influences its parts more in one way and the parts influence the whole more in other ways and a sense in which whole and parts influence each other equally, at least in the sense that both are equally necessary to every whole–part situation.

5. To the extent that whole and parts interact (i.e., causally influence each other): a. Is such causation reciprocal, wholly or partly? b. Is such causation dynamic such that each is changed thereby, or sustained thereby, or both partly sustained and partly changed? c. Is such causation dialectical? That is, is it such that when a part influences a whole which in turn influences that part, the influence received by that part is partly a result of its own influence on the whole? If so, is such causation in some sense, or partly, self-causation by the part? And is it such that when the whole influences a part which in turn influences the whole, the influence received by the whole is partly a result of the whole's influence on the part? If so, is such causation in some sense, or partly, self-causation by the whole?

6. Does every whole–part, or part–whole, situation involve an organic whole (i.e., that whole which includes both the whole as opposed to the parts and the parts as opposed to the whole)? If so, is such organic whole caused to be, and to be what it is, by both the existence and the mutual, including dialectical, interactive causation of the whole and its parts? Does the organic whole itself, then, function in a way that causally influences both the whole and its parts? Is there also interdependence and interaction between the organic whole and the whole and its parts?

7. When one part of a whole causes or is caused by another part

of the same whole, does that part function causally as a part or as a whole in causing or being caused by another part? That is, does each part function as something in itself as well as a part of the whole? Does it have a kind of wholeness of its own, such that its interrelations with the other parts as things has a quality of wholeness about it? If so, does this mean that it too has parts?

8. Further, does the organic whole causally influence other wholes, and does it participate as a part in still larger wholes? These questions receive further treatment in the next chapter, "Levels of Causation."

Whole–Part Causation and Other Categories

Before leaving whole–part causation, let us observe that conclusions about the nature of such causation have implications for other questions, for example, those relative to time, substance, and relations.

TIME.   Insofar as there are wholes and parts of time, or wholes and parts of the temporal aspects of existence, or temporal wholes and temporal parts, how are these interrelated with causation? In discussing time, we illustrated temporal part–whole relationships by days as parts of a whole (lunar) month and months as part of a year, and, if this seems too artificial, then by the heartbeats during a lifetime. The solar system is such that the earth turns on its axis daily, the moon circulates around the earth to complete its phases monthly, and the earth circulates around the sun yearly.

We may ask: Do the days as parts of a month cause the month to be? Do the months as parts of a year cause the year to be? Does the year, as a cycle of the earth about the sun, have a unity or wholeness about it which, so to speak, causes the months, and the days, to be days in such months and such year? Obviously, times (e.g., days, months, and years) are not separate entities but are aspects of eventities. Yet we may focus attention on these aspects and inquire whether a month or a year, insofar as it is a temporal whole, influences its parts? We are aware that in summer the day part of a day–night cycle is longer than it is in winter. Does the completion of a month as a whole influence the days as parts? Thinking only abstractly, or calendar-wise, our answer is likely to be no. But causal interrelations should be more apparent when we are aware that a month is a temporal aspect of a concrete whole: that is, the earth together with its continuing interaction with its moon satellite, within other concrete wholes, such as the sun and its interaction with the earth and other planets.

SUBSTANCE. Substance involves remaining the same through change. Are there wholes of substances as well as substantial wholes? Are there parts of substances as well as substantial parts? Not only may a whole be more or less substantial, and the parts more or less substantial (both individual parts and all of the parts participating in maintaining a whole). The organic whole may be more or less substantial (depending, of course, on the relative substantiality of whole and parts and their continuing interactions). Are substances causes? Are substances caused? Interpreting substances as the substantial aspects of eventities, my answer to both questions is yes.

RELATIONS. Relations are of two or three sorts: external, internal, and organic (i.e., both partly internal and partly external). When the cause of anything is internal to it, we may speak of internal causation. If the parts are internal to a whole, is causation of a whole by its parts internal causation? When parts, each of which is not the other, causally influence each other, is such causation external causation? When a whole causally influences a part, is such causation external or internal? Insofar as the part is not the whole, it is external; but insofar as the part is, functions as, and exists as, a part of that whole, is it not at least partly not only internal to that whole but such that its part–whole relation is an integral part of it?

If doubt remains about this question, consider an organic whole that includes both a whole and its parts. Both whole and parts are internal to the organic whole. But also the organic whole consists mainly of both the whole and its parts and their continuing (i.e., substantial) interaction. Do not both whole and parts also participate in the organicness, the organicity, and the existence of the organic whole? First, the internal relatedness between a whole and its parts and between each part and the whole; second, the external relatedness between a whole and parts and the external relatedness of parts relative to each other; and third, their continuing both internally and externally related in these ways, constitute what is internal to an organic whole. Since such an organic whole functions, additionally, as a part of larger wholes, there is something about it which is also in some sense other than, and thus also externally related to, both its constituent whole and parts.

Immanent and Transcendent Causation

Since we will not explore immanent and transcendent causation elsewhere, we may here raise the question of whether all internal causation is immanent causation and all external causation is transcendent (or transeunt)? Those who draw a sharp line between internal and external will regard these as two distinctly different kinds of causation. But if, as we have seen above, a whole and its parts are both partly internally related to each other and partly externally related to each other, they both involve partly immanent and partly transcendent causation relative to each other. Insofar as a part of a whole that participates as a part in a larger whole, and so on (see below, levels of causation), does such a part participate in some way in several levels of both immanent and transcendent causation?

25 / LEVELS OF CAUSATION

We use the word levels in two different, interrelated, senses.

Levels and Organic Wholes

First, we have already mentioned how a whole of parts is in a sense a higher (i.e., more-inclusive) level of being than each, or even all, of its parts, and how an organic whole, as inclusive of both the whole and its parts, is thus a still higher-level whole. When an organic whole functions also as a part of a larger whole, that larger whole is in a sense a higher-level whole, which together with all of its parts participates in a still-higher-level organic whole. For example, the cells of a heart function as parts of it as a whole, and the cells and heart together function as an organic whole. The heart, as one organ of the body, functions relative to the other organs (e.g., lungs, stomach, skeletal system, muscular system, and nervous system), all of which together serve as parts of the body as a whole. These organs and the body as a whole, through their continuing interaction, serve as a stable basis for the person as an organic whole. A person participating in a society functions as a member or part which, together with the other persons as members, and thus as parts, of that society, contributes to its functioning as a whole. The continuing dynamic interdependence of the members and the society together constitutes that society as another organism, organization, or organic whole.

We could pursue our exploration in the opposite direction, from larger groups, such as nations, down through states, communities, families, persons with bodies and cells, with each cell as a whole composed of molecules of various kinds as parts, each molecule being a whole with various atoms as parts, each of which atom is a whole composed of electrons, protons, and other subatomic particles as parts. Whether or not there is a highest or a lowest level to such a hierarchical series is a question we postpone here. Further treatment of such a hierarchy and of dialectical relations involved in it may be found in chapters 8–11 of my *Polarity, Dialectic, and Organicity*.[1]

We are concerned here with questions of whether and in what ways such a hierarchy of levels involves a hierarchy of levels of causation.

If a part and a whole do not only causally influence each other but do so partly internally, then when such a whole participates as a part in a larger whole and also participates mutually in a partly internal causation with that larger whole, do the part and the larger whole also share any mutual partly internal causation? We assume that, in addition to some external relatedness that holds between a part and its whole and some external relatedness that holds between that whole and a larger whole in which it participates, there is some additional external relatedness between that part and that larger whole. Is there then also some additional internal relatedness and internal mutual causation between that part and that larger whole?

Does the way my heart cells function not only causally influence the functioning of my heart as a whole but also causally influence the way my body functions as a whole and the way I function as a member of my groups? Conversely, does my group-influenced role as worker, boxer, or soldier influence the wear and tear on my body and cause my heart to beat faster which causes my heart cells to respond more actively? Does increased cell activity involve increased molecular, atomic, and subatomic activity? And does the behavior of atoms and molecules, as chemicals, serve to support, as in nourishment, or destroy, as in toxic poisoning, the functioning of my heart, body, and group?

Thus the cell in my heart is both a whole of parts (molecules) which are wholes of parts (atoms) which are wholes of parts (subatomic particles), all of which causally influence its nature and functioning more or less; and it is a part of a whole (my heart) which is a part of a whole (my body) which is a part of a whole (my family) which is a part of a whole (my nation), all of which causally influence its nature and functioning more or less. Causation, in this example, is obviously multileveled. Whether or not all causal situations are such that each cause–effect situation involves multileveled causation doubtless will continue to be debated.

My own hypothesis is that multileveled causation is a universal condition of existence and of each cause–effect situation. How much each such cause–effect situation is influenced by levels more distant, up or down, in the hierarchy is something that needs to be explored on its own account. Sometimes a nation's war policy causes persons to be killed, their hearts and cells to stop functioning, and the molecules and atoms constituting them to disintegrate at least to some extent. And sometimes even an accidental conjunction of chemicals functions as poison which kills cells, heart, body, and person and thus deprives a group of its leader.

Furthermore, just as we have noted that the continuing interaction of a whole and its parts constitutes an organic whole, and that such a whole may also participate in a larger organic whole, we may ask: Is there some limit to the complexity of organic wholes, that is, some limit to the number of levels, and levels of intercausation, that can constitute an organic whole? Or is our solar system also an organic whole? Is our galaxy an organic whole? Is there some largest whole, the universe, that functions as an organic whole, or is there no limit to such a hierarchy? Without attempting to answer this question here, we may at least call attention to the additional complexities involved in the nature of causation revealed here.

Levels and the Nature of Kinds

Second, the question of levels is sometimes intermingled with questions about the nature of kinds. Many philosophers have distinguished kinds of levels of being.[2] Emergentists, for example, distinguish between matter, life, and mind as different levels of being in the sense of different kinds of being. (We shall explore these issues further in the discussion of causation and creativity.) For example, the mind–body problem (which is an entire set of problems) is often conceived in terms of mind and body as two different kinds of being, with the difficulty consequently arising as to how things so different in kind can causally influence each other. We will not pursue the matter further here; but insofar as there are kinds of levels, we may also find kinds of conditions influencing the nature of causation or functioning causally in the hierarchical processes.

26 / CAUSATION AND CREATION

When inquiring into the relations between causation and creation, we discover questions about whether causation and creation are identical, or different, or sometimes identical and sometimes not, or always both identical in some ways and different in others. Answers depend partly on how we choose to use our words.

To cause is to produce an effect. To create is to bring something into existence. If all causation, in producing effects, brings something, i.e., those effects, into existence, all causation is creation. If to create is to bring something into existence, such bringing something into existence is an effect and hence involves causation. So viewed, all causation involves creation and all creation involves causation.

But some causation maintains in existence what is already in existence. The effect caused is continuation of what exists, not bringing something into existence. Such causation does not involve creation, unless such continuation involves the notion of bringing what has existed into being in a new moment of existence. But some things cease to exist and are caused to cease to exist. Does causation that causes a thing to cease to exist, rather than to come in to existence, create? Surely destruction is different from creation; yet both may be caused. So viewed, all creation may involve causation, but causation does not always involve creation.

Creation and Novelty

Another issue is: Does creation involve novelty and, if so, how much? If to create is to bring something into existence, or to cause something to be which did not exist before, is novelty involved? What is brought into existence did not exist before; hence it is a

166

new being. Suppose it is exactly alike, in the sense of being a thing of the same kind as, what existed before. Two coins from the same mold, one made immediately after the other, are different coins and yet exactly alike in kind. How much novelty is required in the coming into being of another thing before we regard it as created? Suppose a coin remains for centuries and one day acquires a new dent; the thing remains the same thing but acquires a new dent. Is such a dent created? Some identify creation with the occurrence of novelty. In this view, all causation that involves novelty is creative. New things can be created, both unique things and things of the same kind. And new characteristics can be created in old things.

But such a view overlooks three features. First, there is not so much difference between new and old as is commonly supposed. Some people easily classify things as new and old: the new generation versus the old generation, new furniture versus antiques, and new clothes versus old clothes. Yet if new means what did not exist before and old means what did exist before, then what is new can last for only a moment. If it lasts for a second moment, it is no longer new but is something which is the same as that which existed before (i.e., at the previous moment); it is already old. The longer what is new exists, the older it is. Yet if what is older lasts for another moment (i.e., a new moment), is it something new in the sense that it now exists at a new moment? Antiques, older people, and older clothes cannot continue to exist at new times without having an element of novelty about them; and new furniture, infants, and new clothes cannot continue to exist without becoming older moment by moment and thus without having an element of aging about them.

Creation and Aging

Second, is aging created? Although aging means remaining the same through the passing of additional times, each such time is a new time. If creation is to bring something into existence, is the bringing of something old into existence at a new time a kind of creation? Recall that time is not separate from events or things (eventities) that change and endure; so the existence of anything at a new or changed time involves it in being a partly new event or thing (eventity); to this extent it involves creation. These considerations do not refute the view that creation involves novelty but appear to refute what some may regard as an implicit notion, namely, that what is new is not old and therefore creativity does not involve either aging or what is old.

Creation and Cessation

Third, when something ceases, it is newly ceased. It involves novel cessation. Do we mean by "creation" bringing some new absence into existence? That is, does every death create a new situation such that the word "create" properly describes it? Or, if novel cessation is not creation, then "creation" cannot be defined merely in terms of novelty. So viewed, it is false that all causation that involves novelty is creative. On the other hand, it may be that a more adequate notion of creativity involves both novelty and aging and both initiation and cessation. We shall try to present such a more adequate view below.

Theories of Causation and Creation

If creation involves both novelty and aging and both initiation and cessation, how is it related to causation? Does causation also involve both novelty and aging and both initiation and cessation? Before we state an affirmative answer, let us review two other theories, namely, one that claims that no genuine novelty and hence no creativity exists, and one that claims that only some causal situations involve genuine novelty and hence creativity.

1. The view claiming that no genuine novelty, and no creativity, exists has been mentioned previously when citing the view that there is as much in the effect as in the cause and as much in the cause as in the effect. The symbolic formula, $C = E$, or cause equals effect, proves very convenient for those attempting to interpret causation mathematically. If there is exactly as much in the effect as in the cause, then there is nothing new in the effect and hence no creation. But, of course, there is also no destruction. "Matter (i.e., matter and/or energy) can be neither created nor destroyed." Hence no genuine creation and no genuine novelty exist. New arrangements, new configurations, new locations, perhaps, but no new existence. (Mechanistic materialists join predeterministic theologians in saying that "there is nothing new under the sun.") But as human knowledge has increased, evidences of genuine novelty have also increased. Process philosophies have become increasingly acceptable to scientific investigators and to philosophers who are aware of newer scientific discoveries.

2. The theory that only some causal situations involve genuine novelty and creativity is called "emergentism." Emergentistic philosophers S. Alexander, C. Lloyd Morgan, R. W. Sellars, and Jan C. Smuts held that from time to time new kinds of being come into existence, for example, when life emerged from matter and when mind emerged from life. In this emergent evolution, they asserted that, though the new kinds of being continue to depend on that from which they emerged (i.e., life on matter and mind on life), they embody new substances, new structures, new properties, capacities, and functions, new laws of behavior, and new centers of causal efficacy.[1]

C. Lloyd Morgan distinguished between "emergents" and "resultants." For example, when one billiard ball is hit by two others, the motion imparted to it is new for it, but the motion, the kind of behavior, is not a new kind of behavior. The amount and direction of motion could have been predicted precisely if the direction and motion of the other two balls had been known. The motion of the ball is explainable as the resultant of the motion of the other two balls.

Emergents involve resultants, but they involve something more. "When carbon having certain properties combines with sulphur having other properties, there is formed, not a mere mixture but a new compound, some of the properties of which are quite different from those of either component. Now the weight of the compound is the additive resultant, the sum of the weights of the components; and this could have been predicated before any molecule of carbon-bisulfide had been formed. . . . But sundry other properties are constituted of emergents which could not be foretold in advance of any instance of such combination."[2]

All causation involves resultants, and to the extent that it does, $C = E$, as with the previous theory. But some causation (i.e., causation that involves emergents and to the extent that it does) involves something new coming into being that did not exist before. There is more in the effect than in the cause in the sense that new substances cause effects in ways that did not exist before. For example, once a mind is caused to emerge in the world, it has capacity to think and imagine and to create ideals and ideas of things that did not exist before. And persons with minds have been able to cause atomic explosions in places, times, and ways which could not have been caused without the causal agency of those minds.

What emerges may demerge. Minds and living bodies die and cease to be. It may be that all minds and all life will disappear from the universe. In such cases, there is less in the effect than in the cause. But while emergents exist, they involve novelty both as effects and novelty as causes. But not all causation involves novelty.

3. Third, let me state my own view. It includes the hypothesis that there is some novelty and thus some creation in every cause–effect situation. There is also some cessation or destruction.

How this appears to be so may be seen by considering what may be regarded as a minimum symbolism for causation. Since, as this hypothesis supposes, every cause–effect situation involves a multiplicity of causes for each effect and a multiplicity of effects of each cause, we need a symbolic picture such as the following.

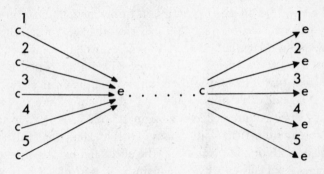

All of the causes, simultaneous and successive, which participate in causing a particular effect, are symbolized by c^1, c^2, c^3, c^4, and c^5. If one thinks of an additional cause which he believes we have not considered, then he may add another c^6 or as many as will satisfy him that the symbols are sufficient to signify all the causes. Now the effect, e, which is caused by all of these causes, is caused by no other causes and is, in this sense, completely caused. There is nothing in the effect that was not caused to be there by the causes, singly and collectively. But notice that, nevertheless, there is something in the effect that did not exist in any of its causes. Insofar as it is an entity or an eventity, it has a unity about it, a unity of its own, that did not exist anywhere previously. "This difference is not only a difference of the effect from each one of its causes taken singly, but also a consequence of the fact that it is one although they are many. That is, c^1 cannot be the sole cause of e, for c^2, c^3, c^4, and c^5 also are its causes. Likewise c^2

cannot be the sole cause of e since it must share such causation with the other causes. Likewise c^3, c^4, and c^5. If e is the joint effect of the five c's there must be something about it which is contained neither in any one of its causes taken singly nor in all of them collectively, because their collectivity involves a manyness, and an external relatedness of each from the others, which does not exist in the effect."[3]

The effect, as an existing entity, in turn functions as a cause of other effects. To the extent that it is caused by its causes, that is, continues in itself what existed in its causes, when it causes effects, it passes on to its effects what it received from its causes. But to the extent that it has a wholeness, unity, or entitiveness of its own, which did not exist in its causes, and which enters into its causal efficacy when it causes effects, it originates new causal efficacy that is different from that of its causes. To the extent that this is so, creation, both of what is novel in the effect and of what is new in the new causal efficacy which originates in it, is involved. According to this hypothesis, then, every causation involves creation, both some new effect and some new cause. Such creation is partial, is aspectival, and is in some cases extremely minute. But in other cases novelty is great, and new kinds of causes are created. All causation involves creation.

Such causation involves destruction also, for in whatever sense each of the causes of an effect had a unity about it which did not continue or recur in that effect, such unity ceased. Whether in the total causal processes in the universe there is exactly as much cessation as creation, I choose not to speculate. (Choosing among the "big-bang" theory of the origin of the universe, the theory that entropy involves a universe that is "running down," the emergentist theory that the universe is building up, and a theory of the universe as pulsating, i.e., both expanding and contracting, I tend to favor the last, although the expanding–contracting aspects of each causal situation interest me more than cosmological speculations.)

My hypothesis further accounts for apparent variations in the loss of and gain in energy apparently present in some kinds of beings by recognizing that causation is also multileveled. That is, for example, when atoms become organized into molecules, the molecular structure and substantial behavior involves energy over and above that constituting the atoms but also conditions, modifies, and incorporates some of their energy into itself as a molecule. A cell is caused to be by other cells in accordance with the causal laws of cell behavior and reproduction. But causal laws, behavior, and creativity involved in molecular causation influence cellular causation and are in turn influenced by cellular causation. A cell in a human body may be caused to come into being to serve the needs of that body, needs caused by a mind's desire to serve a social need such as for blood donation that is caused by a national group's decision to fight a war. That is, a cell may be both an effect of causal processes at molecular, atomic, and subatomic levels and at the same time an effect of causal processes at physiological, psychological, social, and political levels. It may also function causally at all such levels.

Such multileveled causation provides opportunity for greater varieties of novelty and of new creations.[4] It also reveals causality to be much more intricately complex than is usually supposed. And it should discourage efforts to believe that causation can be understood reductionistically by the simple symbolism, $C = E$.

Some today seem to claim that each act of will is *sui generis*. *Existenz*, when "authentic," is spontaneously self-generated. And there are many wills, both those in many persons and those in each person as he wills recurrently.

Thus among philosophers on causation are those who deny any first or originating cause; those who hold that there was only one first or originating cause; and those who claim that there are many independent first or originating causes, whether atomic particles or atomic ("authentic") wills. The view presented here differs from all these in locating first-caused-ness or creativity in every cause–effect situation (as depicted in the previous section). Insofar as there is something novel in each effect (because the effect has and is something in itself that did not exist in its causes) and insofar as that something novel then enters into the causal process (when the eventity occurs both as effect and then as cause), first-caused-ness, or "uncaused-causedness" (if I may use this word to denote something aspectival rather than something existing in isolation) occurs. That is, there appears to be an aspect of creation and of first-caused-ness in all causation. This is all the first-caused-ness, creativity, or "uncaused-causedness," that is needed to account for all creation or for the creation of all novelty.

27 / UNCAUSED CAUSATION

We have yet to explore the problem that is sometimes solved by saying that "there must have been a first cause." For some reason many believe that the view that causation continues perpetually without having begun and without ever ending is unreasonable. They claim that, since nothing happens without a cause, there must have been a first cause. (This argument is sometimes used as proof for the existence of God.) But this claim seems unreasonable to others for, if nothing happens without a cause, then any alleged first cause which happened must itself have been caused. (Mormons accept this argument and hold that God, our Father, had a father [cause] who had a father [cause] who had a father [cause], ad infinitum.)

Yet those who hold that the universe consists of perpetual causal processes that never had a beginning (i.e., a first cause or an uncaused cause) still presuppose that such a universe of perpetual causation is self-contained or self-maintained and thus had no cause outside of itself. Must it, then, not have been uncaused?

In addition to those who hold that there had to be only one first cause, or only one uncaused cause, there are those who hold that there were many first causes. If one believes that the universe consists of indivisible atoms that were never created and can never be destroyed, does he not hold that each, when it enters into causal processes, is a first cause?

This hypothesis received poetic expression by Walt Whitman:

> I have heard what the talkers are talking, the talk of
> the beginning and the end.

175

But I do not talk of the beginning or the end.
There never was any more inception than there is now.
Nor any more youth or age than there is now,
Nor any more heaven or hell than there is now.

The additional issue of determinism versus indeterminism involves first-caused-ness. The determinist says that nothing happens without a cause. The indeterminist says that some things happen without being caused to happen. Thus the indeterminist presupposes uncaused causation. The view presented here proposes that nothing happens without a cause and nothing happens without being caused to happen in the way that it does happen. Yet it also proposes that an aspect of novelty, creation, first-caused-ness, and uncaused causation is present in all causation. But it does not hold that anything can be completely indetermined. It proposes that we are caused to create and, indeed, we are caused to be free. ("Freedom" consists, not in indeterminism, but in being able to do what you want to do. Both abilities and wants are caused.)

What may appear as indeterminacy (e.g., as when one feels himself the author or originator of his own acts of will, which have remained unsatisfactorily explained by attempts to locate physiological and physical causal bases for them) may eventually receive a more satisfactory explanation when we know more about interlevel and multilevel causation. When scientists seek to generalize about causal processes only within one level of existence, such as physical, biological, psychological, or social, and fail to account for causal influences from higher or lower levels, they may be inclined to appeal to "indeterminism." The greater the number of levels (i.e., of different kinds of causes) that cooperate in producing an effect, the more different that effect is likely to be from any one of its causes and from all of them together. So the greater the number of levels from which causal influences come, other things being equal, the more original the effect is likely to be. Greater originality may seem to call for greater indeterminism by one who understands determination all in terms of one level. But according to the hypothesis proposed here, greater originality should be expected when the causes of an effect are both more numerous and, especially, of more different kinds and levels.

28 / CAUSATION AND DESTRUCTION

Too many views, focusing attention on creation and perpetuation, neglect termination, cessation, and destruction. But it may be that destruction is just as common as creation. If so, then an adequate metaphysics will take it into account equally. According to the hypothesis proposed here, both creativity and destructivity are categories of existence: Nothing happens without some creation and some destruction. Beginning and ending, growing and declining, novelty and aging, and thus creation and destruction, are inherent in causation and in existence.[1]

Let us first consider some alternative views. Some hold that the universe, and the things in it, neither were created nor will ever be destroyed. Of these some are materialists who hold that matter neither was created nor is destructible. Some are pantheists who hold God neither was created nor is destructible. Some are Vedantists who hold that Brahman neither was created nor is destructible. Some hold that the universe was created but will not be destroyed. Some hold that the universe never was created but that it is destructible ("The universe is running down"). Some hold that the existing universe is always being created and always being destroyed. A. N. Whitehead proposed that existence consists in "actual occasions" that merely happen (i.e., come into being and go out of being) and that no existing thing endures; hence there are no substances. Some hold that the existing universe is created (manifested) gradually over long periods and is then destroyed (manifestation is withdrawn) gradually over long periods, repeatedly (as the "Days and Nights of Brahman").

Others hold that there are two kinds of beings, those which are

178

neither created nor destroyed and those which are created and destroyed. Another theory is that some things are neither created nor destroyed while other things are destroyed and still others are created but never destroyed ("God is eternal; God created man and the rest of the world; to man he gave eternal life, but the rest of the world is to be destroyed at the end of time").

In contrast with the foregoing, the hypothesis proposed here is that every existing thing (both each event and the "universe as a whole") involves causation and that causation involves some creation, some perpetuation, and some destruction. Probably there is more perpetuation than either creation or destruction in most causation, partly because in a multileveled universe there are as many levels of perpetuation as levels of creation and destruction. Interlevel and multilevel causation involves some maintenance of both the levels and their interdependent interaction.

Just as previously we proposed that there is no causation without creation, so here we propose that there is no causation without destruction. That creation involves causation seems obvious. Does not destruction also involve causation? That is, is not all cessation caused? Or may things just stop being without being caused to stop? Those who hold a doctrine of indeterminism regarding creation may equally well hold to indeterminism relative to destruction or cessation. According to this hypothesis, although there may be an indeterministic aspect of cessation as well as of initiation, all cessation is caused. Just as creation involves novelty and novelty creation, so destruction involves novelty in the sense that something is newly ceased and every new cessation involves destruction. One may raise the question of how, in a cause–effect situation ending in destruction, the cause is something and the effect is nothing. If cause–effect situations were simple, where $C = E$, having $E = 0$ would be unintelligible. But if, as seems to be the case, all cause–effect situations involve many causes and many effects, having some novel cessation as an effect is as reasonable as having some novel creation.

29 / FINAL CAUSATION

Is causing a thing to cease, terminate, end "final causation"? The term "final" has at least two meanings, both of which may be stated in terms of "ends."

Final Causation and Values

One of these meanings is sometimes referred to in terms of values (i.e., intrinsic and instrumental values) or of ends and means. The intrinsic value is the end for which the instrumental values are means. The intrinsic value is the goal of effort to reach it. Some recognize such intrinsic value as present rather than, or as well as, future. Others think of it primarily as something in the future; as such it may have a drawing power, a lure, and even a causal power to prompt effort to achieve it.

Final Causation and Completion

The other meaning of "final" is thought of primarily in terms of time and of temporal termination. According to this meaning, any being that approaches cessation is thereby fulfilling or completing all of its being. Its being is not completed or perfected until its being has ceased; for as long as it has not ceased, there is still some more of it. Its being is fully and finally completed and perfected only when it is ceasing or has ceased to be. Final causation is whatever causes such completion and cessation. Now it may be that, since many causes are involved in such completion, there is a sense in which earlier causes of its development, and even also of its coming into being, are a part of the cause of its completing its being. To the extent that this is so, they are a part of its final causation.[1]

Final Causation and Part–Whole Relations

Another issue often raised relative to final causation deals with the part–whole nature of things. Some hold that when a whole has parts which serve it (cause it to be what it is), they are means to it as an end. Such a whole is conceived of as having, or being, the end for which the parts are means. In such circumstances, causation of the parts by the whole to serve the whole is regarded as final causation. The reason for locating final causation in the whole as against the parts (which may have their own final causation in whatever sense they are wholes of parts) is that wholeness connotes completeness. Although it is true that a thing as a whole does not become temporally complete until it ceases to be, it is nevertheless true also that a whole is a unit that has a temporal unity about it such that it is present as a whole during the passage of all of its temporal parts. The necessity of including the last momentary part in the whole of a thing before it ceases calls our attention to an often-overlooked aspect of finality and final causation. No whole is a complete whole without all of its parts, even though it is from its beginning a whole, and in some sense a whole of all of its parts. (We have yet to explore the issue of potentiality and actuality generally, and specifically relative to a temporal whole and its parts.) In whatever sense it is a whole from the beginning, its functioning as a final cause is already operative. To the extent that it is a complete whole only after including its last part, that last past, involving the act of termination and cessation, is a fundamental part of the location of its final causation.

Part of the significance of the view being presented here is its emphasis on the relative symmetry of first-caused-ness and final-caused-ness as aspects of all causation. Part of this significance is its emphasis on the combined contribution of the wholeness in a whole–parts (organic) situation to both first- and final-caused-ness, where the parts include not merely local particles but causal influences from many levels, higher and lower, to the concrete wholeness that somehow embodies an intrinsic value in its wholeness that comes to its temporal end when that wholeness is perfected and perishes as an entity.

The problem of final causation, causation of what is present by what is future is not a simple one of a distant future goal luring present causal processes in its direction. Final causation operates to cause what is a future part of a present whole to function effectively because such a whole does not cease being a present whole until it includes that future part in its completed (fully finalized) being. But a whole, which has its nature, self-realization, and value within itself as a unit and which is a temporal unit from beginning to end, functions as a final cause because it has its finality within itself. This statement should not prevent us from being aware that some wholes are such that some of their parts somehow "live on after them" or such that these events cause effects (which are "their effects" and hence in a sense parts of them) for many years after. It may be that all "old souls (wholes) never die; they just fade away."

This notion of wholeness and of final causation, which involves each eventity in many levels of interdependence, implies that whatever final causation a whole may have (like whatever first causation may be involved in producing it) is interinvolved not only with its many parts which are also wholes of parts which are wholes of parts, and so on, but also with larger wholes of which it is a part and which are parts of larger wholes, and so on. First-caused-ness and final-caused-ness thus are very intricate conditions of existence and of causation.

30 / CAUSATION AND AGENCY

Can there be causation without a causer? We have not thus far focused on whether a cause, which is different from an effect, is an agent, or an actor, when it causes the effect. We have presumed that causes function agentially without inquiring into the nature of agency, of actors, of acts, of acting, action, and activity, and of enactment. Is every cause an agent? Is every agent a cause?

We can confront our problem immediately by noting that effect is the apposite opposite of cause, whereas patient is the apposite opposite of agent. So far as the agent–patient, or active–passive, relationship is concerned, to be an agent is to act on something else and to be a patient is to be acted on by something else or to be the recipient of action. To be a patient is to be characterized by patience, patiency, or passivity (perhaps even pacifity). The same thing may be both agent in one respect and patient in another. In fact, according to the hypothesis presented here, both agency and patiency are categories of existence. Whatever exists is in some sense a patient and in some sense an agent.

Agency

The question of how a thing acquires agency is not one I can answer in general. The same is true of both existence and all of its categories. Why existence is the way it is, and how it came to have the categories it has, are questions we cannot answer. But in an attempt to understand the nature of its existence, one seeks to discover all of its categories. How a thing acquires agency may escape us; how a thing acquires patiency may not be so obscure. A thing becomes a patient by being acted upon by an agent.

Of course, if somehow a thing cannot be an agent without acting on something else, an agent requires that something else, and depends on its existence and its ability to receive action and its actual receipt of action in order to be an agent. Does this mean that agency originates, at least in part, in the patiency of other things? Do patients somehow activate agents into acting on them? If so, patiency involves its own kind of agency. How this may be so can be seen more clearly when agent and patient are parts of a larger whole whose nature, depending on both, needs both and needs the agency of the agent and the patiency of the patient and hence, as a whole causally influencing its parts, may causally influence the patient to act as a patient and the agent to be the recipient of action of the whole on it in helping it to act as an agent.

Limiting attention to an agent acting on another patient, we may inquire what happens to the patient when it receives the action when being acted upon. Does it "act as patient"? That is, does it function as recipient? Does it *act* as recipient? Can anything *be* a patient without *acting* as a patient? It may be that some things are so patient that their action as patient consists merely in becoming modified as a result, without responding or being activated in any other way. But some things at least seem to respond, or to react, to being acted on. The action on them causes them to react. Such action induces a reaction, and hence action, in the patient. If the thing acted on is not merely momentary but is such that its reaction then also acts on the original actor, that actor becomes a patient. Interaction has started. But in interaction, the original actor becomes a patient, not merely of the action directly from the reacting patient, but indirectly of its own action on that patient. Hence we have here a kind of partial self-causation. The agent is indirectly the partial recipient of his own action.

Introducing self-causation by this indirect manner should call attention to our neglect to consider direct self-causation. Causation is both external and internal. When one thing causes another, each is external to the other. When a thing causes itself, such causation is internal. Now no thing can cause itself, if cause and effect must be partly different from each other, unless such a thing has parts that are at least partially different from each other. (Aquinas' "God as pure act" does not, as Aquinas himself admitted, exist where existence involves time. A purely timeless act is not an act, or, to state it better, no act can be purely timeless, according to the view presented here.) But all things (eventities) do have parts, and all things can and do partly cause themselves and are thus also partly effects of themselves, thus, according to the view presented here, functioning as both agents and patients of themselves.

The difference between internal and external causation, both of which, according to the present view, are categories of existence diminishes when we become aware: (1) that when a thing causes itself even most directly, the difference between it as cause and it as effect is a genuine difference, a genuine otherness, so that an element of externality is inherent in all internal causation because it is inherent in all causation; and (2) that when a thing causes itself indirectly, even most indirectly, by influencing other things which in turn influence it, such causation of itself by itself involves some sameness of itself as both causer and caused which is internal to it as continuing to be the same. I do not wish to diminish this difference too much but wish merely to call attention to it as present in much, if not all, causation and to reveal that here are some more kinds of complications involved in the intricate nature of causation.

Patiency

If every cause involves agency, does every effect involve patiency? Patiency involves being acted on. But are some effects creations of what did not exist before to be acted on? That is, distinguishing between something existing that is acted on when effected and something that is newly brought into being as an effect, the former effect clearly involves patiency, but does the latter kind of effect involve patiency? If the latter kind of effect consisted of a being that was nothing but that effect, then the answer would have to be no. But if the latter kind of effect involves a being which is also more than that effect, such that the effect is something new as a part of something which is also old, then that something, combining the new and old, does function as patient; and so such an effect also involves patiency, even if in a conditional, or aspectival, way.

Distinguishing further between a new cessation or a new absence caused as an effect from both the foregoing something existing which is acted on and something which is newly brought into being as an effect, can the cessation of something be a patient? If the effect of a cause is the cessation of something, that something no longer exists to be acted on and hence cannot, strictly speaking, be a patient. The thing before it ceased is a patient in receiving the effects of the cause that caused it to cease. But after it has ceased, how can it be a patient or involve patiency? If it ceases completely, it cannot. But, according to the view presented here, novel cessation, like novel creation, does not occur in isolation. As long as the absence of what has ceased influences the behavior of other things that were related to it, it has not ceased completely, because, to the extent that some sameness or continuity is involved in all cause–effect situations, that which has ceased as a partially self-existing active agent may still continue to exist partially in its effects in other things. Hence, although to the extent that a thing has ceased, it cannot act as a patient, nevertheless to the extent that a thing which has ceased as self-existing, it may continue to exist in and through other existences. To the extent that there is something in common between what has ceased and what has continued in these ways, that may, then, be said to involve patiency, though in a very conditional, or aspectival, way. For example, at a funeral, the deceased functions as a patient more by virtue of the effects of his death on the mourners than on himself (except, of course, insofar as he continues in some way to be identified with his decaying body). How novelty and cessation may function as having patiency conditionally may be more obvious when we consider both cause and effect as parts of larger wholes, where the whole, at least, is caused to be different by the cessation of the part as contributing somewhat to its continued self-existing.

Immanent and Transcendent Causation

Turning to another distinction, namely, that between "immanent" and "transcendent" causation, let us relate it to internal and external causation. Although whatever is immanent is in some sense internal and whatever is transcendent is in some sense external, something more is involved in each. *Immanent* connotes continuing or remaining. Thus immanent causation is a kind of causation that persists to function causally internally at least. *Transcendent* connotes crossing a boundary or extending over some difference. Limiting our consideration here to immanence and transcendence as apposite opposites, we might observe that, although immanence and transcendence are opposites (the first consisting primarily in something internal and the second consisting primarily in something external), the two have something in common or may be traits, aspects, or parts of something which includes both.

For example, some theologians speak of God as both transcending the world and immanent in the world. The same being, God, is both external to the world and internal to the world and functions both as an external cause, as creator and sustainer, and as an internal cause, as maintainer, either undeviatingly or, some think, acting in special ways (called "miracles"). According to the hypothesis developed here, a whole transcends its parts and functions as a transcendent cause of them, but it is also immanent in each of its parts to the extent that each is, or has as part of its nature, being, a part of that whole.

What is often overlooked is that each part also transcends the whole, not in the sense of being larger than the whole but in the sense that its own nature and being involves something more than its being just a part of that whole and in the sense that, in being both part of the whole and something more than such a part, it crosses over the boundary that would limit it to being just a part of that whole. The part influences the whole both transcendently in whatever sense it is more than a part of the whole and immanently in whatever sense it continues or remains in that whole as a continuing or remaining cause of that whole which includes it as a part. Immanent and transcendent causation thus involve each other. And every whole–part situation (i.e., every organic whole) involves both in at least one way and probably in many ways. Where multilevel causation is involved (and where is it not?), many varieties of immanent and transcendent causation are present.

Returning now to agency, does every agent involve both immanent and transcendent causation? Perhaps the easiest way to answer this question is by asking another: Does all causation (i.e., every cause–effect situation) involve both immanent and transcendent causation? If cause and effect are partly the same and partly different, does that part of the cause which remains the same in the effect function as immanent causation as long as the effect continues to be determined by it, and does that part of the cause which causes the effect to be different from the cause function as transcendent causation as long as the effect continues to have such difference determined by it? If all causation involves both immanent and transcendent causation, and if to be an agent is to be a cause, then every agent is involved in both.

What about patiency? Insofar as an effect involves patiency, and insofar as an effect is the same as its cause, is not the cause immanent in the thing that is affected as patient? Insofar as an effect involves patiency and insofar as an effect is different from its cause, which continuing difference was caused in it by its cause, does not the cause continue to function as a transcendent cause? Insofar as an effect involves patiency, it involves something that is both patient and more than patient relative to such an effect; that something transcends such effect, by both including it as a constituent and existing as more than it. If such something becomes a reagent and reacts relative to that which was the cause, so that interaction occurs, agency and patiency and immanent and transcendent causation become involved in dialectal developments that constitute more complicated aspects of causation.

31 / CAUSATION AND POWER

What is power? I do not know. But we observe that some things are able to cause effects and other things, or the same things at other times, apparently are not able to cause effects. Thus we infer that sometimes ability to cause effects is present and sometimes it is not. We can refer to power as the ability to cause effects. Powers, and causes, are of four general sorts: (1) power to cause change or difference to become, (2) power to cause permanence or remaining the same, (3) power to resist change or to remain the same when influenced by causes, (4) power to become different when influenced by causes.

1. Power to change, or to make a difference, is itself of many kinds. Two obvious kinds are the power of one thing to cause a change in other things and the power of one thing to cause a change in itself. The effects may be a new existing difference in the same existing thing, a new kind of existing difference in other existing things, a new cessation of an existing thing, or even a new cessation of a kind of existing thing (whole species may be caused to become extinct).

2. Power to cause permanence, or remaining the same, is of two kinds: first, the power of one thing to perpetuate itself and, second, the power of one thing to support the endurance of other things; or the power of an agent to continue its agency and the power of an agent to perpetuate its patients.

3. Power to resist change, or to remain unchanged, is of two kinds: first, the power of a thing to resist internal changes and, second, the power of a thing to resist external changes.

4. Power to become different, or changed, is of two kinds: first,

the power of a thing to become modified as a result of its own causes and, second, the power of a thing to become different as a result of receiving effects from external causes.

These four kinds of power are not so different from each other as a formal analysis makes them appear. If we recall that time exists, or is an aspect of all existence, then we can observe that the power to cause permanence is a power to cause something to exist at different times and that the power to remain unchanged is a power to exist at different times. Temporal differences are involved in all remaining the same. On the other hand, to the extent that a cause is in some sense the same as, or continuous with, its effects, we can infer that the power to cause change, or difference to become, must also somehow be somewhat the same as, or continuous with, its effects. Also, the power of a thing to perpetuate itself and the power of a thing to resist change or to remain unchanged are completely different only if two such things exist in isolation. But if, or since, all things exist in relation with (and usually in interaction with) other things, these two powers themselves constantly cooperate, or rather are two aspects or functions or parts of some fuller power of a thing as agent–patient.

To the extent that a whole depends on its parts, its parts act as causal agents with power to support the whole. To the extent that a part depends on a whole, that whole acts as a causal agent with power to sustain the part. To the extent that the parts of a whole depend on each other, both for their support of that whole and, indirectly, for their support by the whole, each acts as a causal agent with power to support each other. Their mutual causation, of whole and parts and of parts by each other, functioning stably together, participates in causing the maintenance of the organic whole consisting of all of them. To the extent that such organic whole functions as a part of a still larger whole and, further, in several levels of larger wholes, it (and its mutually caused whole-and-parts) functions causally in that large whole and in the several levels of larger wholes; and it is (and its mutually caused whole-and-parts are) causally affected by that larger whole and by its participation in several levels of larger wholes. According to the present hypothesis, the same is true of lower levels within the parts. The powers of these parts and wholes to cause change and to become changed and to remain the same and to resist change intermingle variably. Recognition of such variations is needed for full comprehension of the nature of causation and of power.

32 / CAUSATION AND POTENTIALITY

Complexities in the nature of causation and power may be explored further by examining the distinction between power to cause which has not yet caused and power to cause which has caused. Issues involved here usually receive attention under the heading "potentiality versus actuality." Potentiality, or potency, is power to become. It is power to cause the becoming of something actual, the power to actualize, or the power to cause actualization. Actuality, on the other hand, is whatever exists actually. Relative to potentiality, actuality is that which has come into being, that which has become, that which has been actualized, or that which exists because it has been caused to be by whatever powers caused it to come into being.

Potentiality

An important, although sometimes neglected, aspect of potentiality is the power not merely to come into being but also to remain in being. Such power to remain in being is a power to continue to come into being in each new relevant unit of time. Another even more neglected aspect is the power to cease being, or to become actually not. Whether potentiality should be regarded also as power to remain actually not will depend on whether, and to what extent, such being not is also not being. Being not is a kind of being whereas not being is not a kind of being. Being not involves the being of something which is negated in some way. If anything becomes not actually by ceasing to be something, that cessation occurs in an existing situation where what is actual exists without it (i.e., with it as out or as not present). In this way some potentiality is power to cease being or to become actually not. How long something can remain actually not is interesting to speculate about. But that some things remain actually not longer than others may be illustrated by a familiar example. Some students drop a course on the last day of the semester; some are dropped after three absences; some cease coming the second day but continue to be regarded as absent members until the end of the semester.

Actuality

"Actuality is prior to potency."[1] The power of anything to become must exist in something that already exists or is actual. Only what is actual has potentiality or power to become. No nonactual potentiality exists in the sense that there are no potentialities apart from actualities. Yet to the extent that what is actual could not have become actual without the power that caused it to be actual, such power is causally prior to its existence as actual. Hence in one way actuality is prior to potentiality and in another way potentiality is prior to actuality. Each is prior in its own way.

"To be actual, it has also been held, is to be effective."[2] To be actual, some say, is to be active; and to be active is to be actual. To be active is to act as an agent and to cause an effect. Thus not only is all potentiality existent only in what is actual but also all that is actual not only is potential, or has potentiality, but also is active in causing effects or in actualizing its potentialities. Some hold that what is actual must actually be causing, or even have caused, other effects to be actualized; others hold that what is actual may merely exist without yet causing or having caused anything to be actualized. My view is that there are two aspects of actuality, one consisting of its being actual or in existing and the other consisting of its potentiality or power to cause actualization of what is not yet actual. How much what is actual is already acting in realizing its potentialities to actualize will be explored further when we consider time and whole–part causation.

Conditional Potentiality and Real Potentiality

The nature of power and potentiality cannot be fully comprehended apart from a distinction between two kinds of potentiality, "conditional potentiality" and what we stipulatively term "real potentiality." By "conditional potentiality" we mean the power which anything has that could cause a particular effect if all other conditional potentialities needed to produce it would cooperate. By "real potentiality" we mean all of those powers (i.e., all of those conditional potentialities) which do in fact cooperate in the production of something that becomes actual. An acorn, for example, has the capacity to cause the existence of an oak tree, but only if other things with other capacities, such as water, nutrients, sunlight, proper temperatures, absence of destructive competition, and time, also cooperate in causing the existence of the oak tree. It may be that some things have within them all the power needed to actualize their potentialities. The universe, for example, must have such power, if there is such a thing as the universe. And some simplest cause, such as a long-enduring thing at one moment and the same thing at the next moment, may have in it all the power needed for such actualization. But according to the view presented here, all things (including the universe) interdepend, that is, depend on other things as well as have some independence of other things. Therefore, each effect actualized is caused by many causes (i.e., many powers, or many potentialities, and potentialities at many levels of existence).

Most, if not all, things are caused by other things with potentialities not all of which are realized or actualized. Although, on the one hand, "... it cannot be true to say 'this is capable of being but will not be' ...,"[3] on the other hand, this is true only of what we have called "real potentialities." It is true that an acorn which did not grow into an oak tree did not have the capacity (i.e., sufficient capacity) to do so. Yet there is something about an acorn that could grow into an oak tree if other things would cooperate, and it has this conditional capacity whether or not such capacity is actualized. An acorn does not have the potentiality of becoming actualized as a maple tree or a tomato plant. It has an impotence, impotency, or impotentiality, inherent in its actuality. Impotence is a genuine characteristic of actualities and, according to the hypothesis presented here, of all actualities. Each thing (eventity, actuality) has both potentiality and impotentiality; it has power to become something else, but it does not have the power to become everything else.

Whatever it becomes, or causes to become, depends partly on other things in order to bring about whatever it causes. Its power together with other powers cooperate in actualizing whatever becomes actual. Powers which it has to actualize a kind of thing when other needed powers do not cooperate remain merely potential. Not only are there specific kinds of impotentiality (an acorn cannot become a maple tree), but there are also general kinds of impotentiality: all those situations in which conditional potentialities lack cooperation by other conditional potentialities needed for actualizing a specific kind of thing (acorn cannot become an oak tree merely by its own powers).

I disagree with Aristotle's view of potentiality as consisting in essence or essential form. The potentiality ("real potentiality") causing the actualization of anything consists of all the powers actually cooperating in its production. To select some conditional potentialities, such as an acorn that has a conditional potentiality of becoming an oak tree, and to assert that they are the potentiality of what becomes an actual oak tree is to speak falsely. Part of the powers contributing to the actualization of an oak tree, no matter how essential, are not all of the powers. If water, nourishment, and the like are essential to the actualization of an oak tree, they are parts of *the* potentiality that produced it. Furthermore, whereas Aristotle appears to have regarded some actual conditions participating in causing an oak tree as "accidental" rather than "essential," I view all such actual participating causes as part of *the* potentiality of what is produced. It is true that things which become actual are of different kinds, and kinds of potentiality are essential to their production. But as long as variations in the kinds of conditions (conditional potentialities) occur in the production of things of any kind, those varying conditions are parts of *the* potentiality actualizing a particular thing of that kind.

Relation to Cause and Effect

If potentiality and actuality are related to causality in such a way that potentiality is power in something actual to cause, "conditionally" or "really," the actualization of something else, and that actuality is whatever exists as a consequence of being caused to exist by the powers that produced it and has power to cause, "conditionally" and "really," something else, then they interdepend. Each is not the other. "Let actuality be defined by one member of this antithesis, and the potential by the other."[4] Yet each depends on the other and both are aspects of every existent. No actuality exists without potentiality, both that which produced it and that which it has as productive. No potentiality exists without actuality, for, on the one hand, only that which is actual is or has potentiality and, on the other hand, all actualities have potentialities which do cause other actualities even if not all of the conditional potentialities actualize things of the same kind. There are, also, no impotentialities apart from actualities, and every actuality has impotencies also. Causation is complicated by actuality–potentiality, potency–impotency, and conditional–real potentiality polarities.

Does every cause–effect situation involve all of these polarities? Is every cause both potential and actual, both conditionally and really, in producing its effect, and also impotent in the sense that it cannot, really, produce any effect which it does not produce? Is every effect both potential and actual, both conditionally and really, in its production, and also a product of impotence to cause it to be different from the way it was produced? My hypothesis proposes a yes answer to the two questions and postulates the involvement of both some novelty, some remaining the same, and some cessation in each cause–effect situation. All are categories of existence.

Let us inquire how whole–part causality relates to our actuality–potentiality, and so on, polarities. In contrast to those views which hold that parts have their potentiality completely in the prior actuality of a whole and to those views which hold that the whole consists merely in a sum of its parts (potentiality causing the whole has its being completely in the prior actuality of the parts), the hypothesis proposed here is that every whole–part situation involves many kinds and levels of actuality, potentiality, and impotency. In every whole–part situation, whole and parts interdepend, each causally supporting and being supported by the other. Each (i.e., both the whole and all its parts), is part of the power that causes the others to continue their participation. Each such part of the power is a potentiality ("real potentiality") actualized in the continuing interaction and interdependence of the part–whole situation (organism) and in turn of the continuation of each such part.

When we observe further the higher and lower levels of whole–part participation, we become aware of many levels of actuality, potentiality, and impotence. A full account of *the* potentiality producing any actuality, which avoids the fallacy of simple location, will recognize many levels of potentiality and impotentiality.

I refrain from speculating whether there is some inverse square in the ratio of the relative power which more distant (higher or lower) potentiality has in constituting the potentiality of whatever is actualized.

Relation to Time

Let us conclude our consideration of causation and potentiality by relating them to time with its events and duration, its presents, pasts, and futures, its parts and wholes, and its levels. If what is present is actual and what is actual is present, and if some presents last longer than others, does some of what is actual last longer than other actualities? For example, insofar as several heartbeats during one inhalation, or several (twenty-eight) days during one (lunar) month, function as parts of wholes, due to their interdependent functioning as parts of a human body or of a planetary system, are the present heartbeats, inhalation, days, and month all actual? Assuming some unity essential to the existence of each, such that each remains actual from its beginning to its end, several heartbeats become actual and cease being actual before the actual inhalation ends its actuality, and several days become actual and cease being actual before the actual month ends its actuality. If there are also still higher levels of actuality, such as a present year, present existence of our solar system or of our galaxy, and still lower levels of actuality, such as those of present atoms and subatomic particles, actuality has amazing complexities, to say the least.

Since, according to the present hypothesis, a month and the days of a month do interdepend, we can say that yesterday, which is no longer actually present as the present day, is *actually* past as a day in the present actual month. Likewise, tomorrow, which is not yet actually present as the present day, is *actually* future as a future day in the present actual month. Yesterday has no actuality merely by itself, but, by having caused the present actual month to have aged by one more day, it continues to function in its present effects in the month as actual. But, then, today also has no actuality merely by itself either. True, it does have its own actuality, but it is also a part of the actuality of the present month. If each thing is involved in both kinds of actuality, its own while it has its own existence as present and its actuality as participating in the actualities of other things, then it has more actuality than many thinkers will admit. To the extent that a thing participates in still higher-level wholes, it involves, because it is involved in, higher-level actualities.

Turning from actuality to potentiality, the power of each thing, such as a day (or that complex organism of which a day is an aspect), to participate in, and causally support, some larger whole, such as a month, first as tomorrow, then as today, and then as yesterday, involves not only whatever power it has within itself to function as an actual today but also the power which the month (or that complex organism of which the month is an aspect) has to cause the day to come into being actually both as tomorrow, today, and yesterday. Its potentiality while it is still tomorrow may depend more on, and be constituted more by, the power of larger actual wholes than by any potentiality belonging to its own actuality which does not yet exist as today. Such potentialities are not no potentialities and are its potentialities in whatever way it is caused to become actual by them. When it becomes actual, it in turn serves as part of the potentiality for completion of the month, for the coming of the next tomorrow, and for its own becoming actually past.

Such temporal conditions of overlapping actualities and multi-leveled potentialities constitute parts of causation as a category of existence.

33 / CAUSAL LAWS

When the word "causation" is used, many persons immediately think of causal laws. So much of the discussion about causation focuses on such laws that issues regarding the metaphysical conditions of such laws, for example, those conditions discussed in the previous chapters, tend to be ignored. Difficulties with attempts to discover and formulate causal laws have led many to give up attempts to understand laws of nature and many to give up trying to understand the nature of causation.

What Is a Law?

We may distinguish four kinds of "laws": laws of nature, scientific laws (formulated as hypotheses or theories about laws of nature), laws of logic and mathematics (i.e., of abstracted or postulated deductive systems), and legislated laws (politically agreed on or promulgated). Discussion here will be limited to laws of nature or laws of existence. Formulation of scientific laws belongs to the study of theory of knowledge, inductive logic, philosophy of science, or what these three have in common.

Laws of nature are simply whatever uniformities exist together. If a universal consists in any sameness of (all of) two or more things, then, minimally, a law consists in one sameness between two existing universals. For example, when visiting an ancient ruin, I bump my head on a low doorway twice, once going in and once coming out. The presence of the low doorway was the same on the two occasions and so constituted a universal. Bumping my head was the same on both occasions and so constituted a universal. The conjunction or correlation of the low doorway and bumping my head on both occasions constituted a law. I can formulate the law "scientifically" by saying that, "All occasions in which I passed through this doorway are also occasions in which I bumped my head." The example is trivial, but it serves to illustrate, minimally, an existing law.

Most laws in which we become interested are much more complicated. They tend to involve not only multiplicities of occasions but also many different samenesses. Even the above example may be observed to involve more complexities, such as failure to lower my head, failure to notice the height of the doorway, being as tall as I was, standing erect, and so on, on both occasions, and thus to involve other universals and correlations between them.

If, as we have proposed, there are categories of existence, then each occasion in the above example also involved the copresence of all of them also. Between categories of existence there is a complete correlation, so such correlations constitute metaphysical laws or categoreal laws. That is, such laws are themselves categories of existence. If space and time are both categories of existence, then the correlation, or copresence, of space and time is also a category of existence. Then the universal presence of space whenever there is time and the universal presence of time wherever there is space are two categoreal laws of existence.

What Is a Causal Law?

A causal law exists, minimally, whenever (all of) two cause–effect occasions are alike in any respect. That is, given a cause that produces an effect and another cause that is like it and produces a like effect, we have a correlation or likeness between the two causes and between the two effects. The recurrence of this correlation or likeness is a law.

Recalling the foregoing example (describing the correlation of going through a low doorway and bumping my head on two occasions as a law), let us now observe further that bumping my head was caused. I cannot know all of the causes, since causal factors included whatever reasons the ancients had for building the doorway in the first place, conditions enabling perpetuation of the doorway throughout the centuries, factors in my biological ancestry that resulted in my height, and motives leading me to visit the ruin. But let me select one factor that contributed causally to the bumping, namely, my failure to lower my head. My failure to lower my head on the two occasions caused me to bump my head twice. The copresence of this failure on (all of) both occasions as a causal factor is sufficient for the presence of an existing causal law.

Again the triviality of minimal conditions for the existence of a causal law may seem to some as insufficient. But if we can understand laws, and causal laws, in their simplest forms, then we should be able to understand them better when more complexities are observed. I believe that it is humanly impossible to give a complete account of all of the causal factors contributing to even the simple recurrence of bumping my head twice on one doorway. But the hypothesis that nothing happens (exists) without being caused to happen (i.e., that causality is a category of existence) does not seem to be unreasonable as a continuingly reliable working hypothesis in metaphysics.

If each cause–effect occasion involves as categoreal factors all the characteristics considered in the foregoing chapters, then they too may be observed to be present as factors in every other existing causal law that may be observed. If, as proposed here, existence is inherently dialectical, then dialectic may also be observed as present as part of every causal law.

Discovery of specific causal laws present in specific kinds of existences is a matter for the specific empirical sciences to investigate. But if the characteristics that have been proposed here as categories of existence are actually categoreal, then investigators in each of the specific sciences should be able to observe them also as present conditions.

PART THREE

DIALECTIC

34 / WHAT IS DIALECTIC?

Dialectic, originally meaning dialogue with give and take between discussants, has been extended to give and take between existing things.

As dialogue between two persons, dialectic involves each thinker in communicating to the other ideas which add to the other's information in such a way that it becomes incorporated in his reply. Then the response of the first person to the second person's reply likewise not only continues to express somewhat the same ideas which the first already communicated but now is modified by ideas originating in the other when he replied. The thinking in each discussant grows, not merely through the receipt of ideas from the other, but through ideas stimulated in each partly by the other. Each, first enriched by ideas from the other, further enriches the other through adding his own modifications. Each progressively embodies more of the other's thoughts within himself.

As dialectic between two existing things, events, or processes, dialectic involves each of the things in causally influencing the other in such a way that each develops through such interaction. That is, each, while remaining the same in some fundamental ways, changes not only as a consequence of influences by the other but also as a consequence of influences by the other which have been somewhat influenced by itself. Thus, the development of each, in a give-and-take situation, is a product partly of what each takes from the other after the other has been modified by what each has given the other. In this interchange, each develops partly in response to his own influences on the other. Each evolves through a kind of self-development that uses the other as a means for self-modification.

However, prolonged dialectic becomes substantial, thereby creating a third thing or "synthesis" which preserves the mutuality that has developed between the two. The more the self-development of each of two things, or persons, depends on such continuing dialogue, the more such mutuality becomes and remains stable as something in itself.

Although nothing is more common, in human or animal communication and in interactions between other existing things, than dialectic, some simple but subtle aspects of dialectic seem to exclude it from our attention, partly, I suspect, because we develop an interest in clarity of distinctions whereas certain aspects of dialectic can never be made completely clear. On the one hand, dialectic is an ever-present condition of existence, including existing communication; yet, on the other hand, we habitually ignore it when we seek to understand by merely analytic means. Dialectic involves each participant in retention and growth of its own wholeness through recurrent partial influences. Analysis that yields only parts ignores the continuing role of wholeness in both existers and knowers.

Each communicator is involved in dialogue with all others with whom he communicates, and each thing is involved in dialectic with all other things with which it is interrelated. Hence a thinker and his society and a thing and its environment (e.g., electron and field) engage in very complex interactions and intricate self-developments on the part of each of the participants. If analysis fails to capture comprehension of retention of evolving wholenesses on the part of two dialecticians, it fails even more to yield comprehension of retention of wholeness through interactions with multiplicities of dialecticians. Those baffled when trying to understand wholeness by analytical methods often surrender either to agnosticism or to mystical intuition. Yet only a little effort to comprehend and practice understanding through awareness of the existence and nature of dialectic may reveal it as an omnipresent feature of existence as experienced. Dialectic, according to the hypothesis presented here, is a category of existence.

35 / INGREDIENTS IN DIALECTIC

Dialectic involves not merely (1) one thing (thesis, posit), but (2) many things in such a way that (3) each is opposed (antithetical, opposite) to one or more others (4) directly (appositely, i.e., with respect to something which they share in common, such as kind or dimension) and to others indirectly (as inapposite opposites).

For example, a man and a woman are apposite opposites because, both being human, they share humanity in common. A man and a mare are inapposite opposites. A day as an event and as a duration has eventness and duration as apposite opposites because they share temporality in common. A day as tending (i.e., aiming) to complete itself, and as having such completion as its natural goal, has aimingness and goalness as apposite opposites because they share purposiveness in common. The duration and goalness of a day are also opposites but, being different in kind, are inapposite opposites. A whole and its parts are apposite opposites, but here one whole (as thesis) has many parts (antitheses) as apposite opposites; or each of many parts (theses) is appositely opposed to its whole (antithesis). They are apposite because they share organic wholeness in common.

(5) Apposite oppositeness, at least, involves polarity. That is, each is both something positive (a thesis) and oppositive or negative (an antithesis), with respect to something (a kind or dimension), which they share in common. Furthermore, each depends on the other for the existence and continuation not merely of that which they share in common but for its own perpetuation. Although a particular man or woman might live out his or her life in isolation

from others, if either all men or all women became extinct, apparently there could be neither humanity nor other men nor other women. If time involves both events and duration, then elimination from existence of either all events or all duration would eliminate all time, and all other polar (events or duration) ingredients in time.

(6) Thus polar opposites depend on each other for part of their nature (both for what each shares in common with the other and for being the complementary opposite needed to complete what is shared) and their existence. But polar opposites also have some independence of each other, for as antitheses, each is and has something that the other does not. Women have something that men do not and vice versa; each has something the other does not. The independent aspects of the being and nature of two antitheses are just as essential to their polar nature as is their mutual dependence on each other. Polar opposites interdepend.

(7) That which polar opposites (antitheses) share in common also functions as something in itself (a synthesis). For we recognize that not only are men and women opposites, but also that humans and tigers are opposites (antitheses), especially when they meet in a struggle for existence. Not only are events and duration opposites, but time is opposed to space. When we observe time and space as antitheses, time functions as a thesis even though it is also a synthesis of events and duration.

(8) Although a synthesis of two antitheses is often spoken of as a "new thesis," the newness of a higher-level thesis as higher occurs only in synthetic dialectic in which the synthesis results from a process of integration of two antitheses. A new thesis may result also from analytic dialectic,[1] which we shall discuss later. Not all higher-level theses come into existence as new theses emerging from previously existing antitheses, because some kinds of hierarchy are inherent in the nature of some complex kinds of things from their very beginning. For I think that we did not first have a woman and then a man, or, as in the biblical account, first a

man and then a woman, or even both a woman and a man, and then humanity. Men, women, and humanity emerged into being together, I suspect.

(9) *Hierarchy* is the name we give to the existence of higher and lower levels of theses. Higher-level theses may result from antitheses functioning together through syntheses. Lower-level theses may result from wholes functioning as theses within which, or from which, new parts emerge as new things or theses ("partitheses," or "analytheses").[2] Doubtless each thing participates in a multileveled hierarchy. And if, as we propose, existence is dynamic, then each thing participates, even if somewhat indirectly, in many levels of dialectical development.

(10) Dialectic is processual; so process is inherent in, or is an ingredient in, dialectic. Since process involves time, dialectic is temporal. It involves change, including the emergence of novelty and both aging and cessation. Its processes are of various kinds, for through it some things are perpetuated longer and others cease sooner. Through it things may become larger or smaller, more rigid or more flexible, more the same or more different, more complex or perhaps more simple. Some theses proceed dialectically primarily by becoming subordinated to other theses, some by subordinating other theses, and some by largely destroying their antitheses and incorporating such within themselves through progressive synthesis.

For example, consider myself and an apple as antitheses. I eat the apple, a bite at a time. Such eating is a dialectical process. The apple is other than myself. I bite, chew, and swallow part of the apple. When I take the next bite, what I swallowed of the first bite is already a part of my body and hence of myself. To the extent that this is true, the first-bitten part of the apple participates in me as I take the second bite. It would be foolish to say that the apple is thereby biting itself, and yet there is a sense in which this is true. (If one believes that digestion and absorption of molecules into the body tissues are required before they function as part of body and self, then an example of refrigerated deer meat eaten over a period of months may seem more obvious.)

After I have eaten the entire apple, the apple as my antithesis has ceased to exist except insofar as it continues on within me as a participant in me as a synthesis of my self previous to eating it and it as digested and absorbed. If I cannot survive without eating again and again and again, then I must destroy, partly or completely, those things (antitheses) that I consume as food. By incorporating each such thing within me, I become progressively more synthetic. Of course, I also excrete, exhale, sweat, and consume energy by exercising, thereby bringing parts of myself either to cessation or to separate (antithetical) existence. Thus each person, even merely as a survivor, is a very complex system of dialectical processes.

Although the consumed apple is destroyed as a thing or thesis, if my survival depends on eating other apples, and if I cannot eat other apples without caring for the growth of apple trees, then apples as a kind of thing (species) may benefit because I thereby seek to plant, fertilize, water, and protect such apple trees. When kinds of theses mutually serve each other, even though particular theses of each kind is partially consumed by the other, each may survive longer as a consequence of their mutual services. The conclusions of ecological scientists, and the current popular clamor about pollution and overpopulation, dramatize dialectical interdependencies of human beings and their complex environments.

(11) Implicit in the foregoing discussion is the variety, seemingly endless variety, of kinds of dialectic. If, as is contended here, dialectic is a category of existence, there are as many varieties of dialectic as there are varieties of existing things. In the foregoing we have distinguished several varieties of synthetic dialectic, such as a man and woman as antitheses functioning jointly in a family as a new thesis, a person eating an apple as an antithesis which then functions in the person as an enlarged synthesis, and a kind of thing (species) as a synthesis of its members.

Physical dialectic may be exemplified by the gravitational attraction of two bodies, for example, two huge stones which, in the absence of counter attractions, may move toward each other gradually over a long period. If the force of gravity increases inversely with the square of the distance between the two bodies, then any unit of distance that increases the gravitational attraction by one unit of force (quantum of energy) thereby dialectically makes the same stone and its gravitational pull grow by incorporating one more (antithetical, i.e., before added) unit to force within itself.

Each additional wave of any kind of wave series may be thought of as antithetical before it is incorporated into the series. The seeming contradictions between the wave and particle theories of light disappear when light is viewed as dialectical in nature; for the particle pole of a wavicle (wave-particle) is the permanent aspect of a thesis that continues to be permanent only by continuing to add, and thus incorporate into itself as continuing, each successive wave.

(12) Incompleteness is another characteristic of dialectic, because it is another characteristic of existence. Or perhaps I should say that existence and dialectic are characterized by a complete–incomplete (finite–infinite, finished–unfinished) polarity. For everything that has existed and no longer exists has completed its existence. And not only all things that have existed have completed, but all things that will exist will eventually complete, their existence. Also, everything that is still existing has not completed its existence and thus is unfinished and, in this sense, infinite. Although each existing thing (thesis) will eventually complete itself and cease to be (according to the view proposed here), existence and the categories of existence including dialectical process will continue unendingly. Insofar as each thing, even after it has ceased to be as a thing, continues on through its effects upon, and interrelations with, including its being not, other things that continue, it too continues on, in this aspectival way, unceasingly.

Such incompleteness is described by some pragmatists as "an

open future." Even Hegel's "The Absolute," if I interpret him correctly, is idealized as perfectly complete; but it can be so only by including all of time, not only all future time but also an endless future.

(13) If, as we propose, dialectic is a category of existence, then exploration of the interrelations of dialectic and all other categories of existence should reveal them as ingredients. In the following survey, we will focus more on the categories as polar opposites than on existing things, but since, according to the view presented here, the categories of existence have no being or nature independent of existing things, the interrelations of dialectic and other categories make them ingredients in it only as dialectic existing in things.[3]

36 / DIALECTIC AND OTHER CATEGORIES

Consideration of other categories here will be limited to samples of polar pairs treated in parts one and two.

Sameness and Difference

DIALECTIC INVOLVES SAMENESS AND DIFFERENCE. It does so in several ways. Each thing both remains partly the same and becomes partly different as a consequence of participating in dialectical interactions. My self before and after asking you a question and receiving an answer is largely the same self; yet new information received from you causes me to be somewhat different. My wife and I both embody something in common as a consequence of our sharing a marriage relationship with each other; but we are also both different as a consequence of our marriage, for neither is now open to marriage proposals by others. As joint owners of property we function as a unit, for property tax purposes, for example. Each of us, as a thesis, is not the other and hence is an antithesis. Yet by sharing in a marriage, we embody a common dimension; and by acting as joint property owners, we function together as a new thesis.

SAMENESS INVOLVES DIALECTIC. For sameness exists only when two or more things are the same in some respect, and one thing cannot be the same as another unless the other reciprocates by being the same as the one. When two things are the same in some respect, each thing is a thesis and also, in being not the other thing, is an antithesis. And each, by being the same as the other in this respect, contributes something to the other that it cannot contribute by itself, namely, the sameness which the other has with the one. Without both the sameness embodied in the one and in the other, the sameness common to both could not exist. That sameness, once existing, functions as a common dimension constituting the two things as things of a same kind, or a new thesis. Thus sameness existing in its minutest form already involves dialectic.

DIFFERENCE INVOLVES DIALECTIC. For two things that are different differ in one or more respects. Two things differing in only one respect function both as theses, in being things, and as antitheses, in being both different things and differing from each other in that respect, and yet also are alike relative to that respect. For when things differ in any respect, such as being longer or shorter, that respect, length, is something they have in common; or such as being black and white, that respect, color, is something they have in common; or such as being a mouse and a star, that respect (i.e., being different kinds of things) has "difference in kind" in common. If "difference in kind" functions also as "a kind of difference," it functions as a "new thesis." If so, then difference existing in its minutest form already involves dialectic.

Change and Permanence

DIALECTIC INVOLVES CHANGE AND PERMANENCE. Each of two interacting theses influences the other, thereby changing it; and is influenced by the other, and thereby is changed itself; and influences itself indirectly through influencing the other to influence it, and thereby is self-changed. When a new dimension emerges from the stability of their interaction, change is involved in the coming into being of this new dimension. When the two function as a new thesis, change is again involved in the coming of what is new.

Permanence is also involved in such dialectic. For each of the two theses also remains in some respects the same, and hence permanent, through all such changes. Stability in both the new dimension shared by both and the new thesis through which both function involves permanence.

CHANGE INVOLVES DIALECTIC. For each change involves both something before the change and something after the change which are both different (from *is not* to *is,* or from *is* to *is not,* or both) and also the same, for as an event, a change is a unit and is somehow the same from beginning to end. Taking "something before the change" and "something after the change" as antitheses, and "the change" as the synthesis or new thesis, both the "before the change" and the "after the change" then function thetically in whatever way the change itself influences the future course of events.

PERMANENCE INVOLVES DIALECTIC. For to be permanent is to remain the same through change. Such remaining the same is only a partial sameness, since, unless that which is permanent and that which is changing exist somehow in complete isolation from each other, the relations between them are such that what exists as permanent during one change is somewhat different from that which exists as permanent during another change. Hence to continue as permanent a thing must synthesize both its remaining the same through change and its becoming different through such change.

Wholes and Parts

DIALECTIC INVOLVES WHOLES AND PARTS. For whatever is involved in dialectic is an existing thing or thesis which, as *an* or *one,* has a unity or wholeness about it. But according to the view presented here, each thing consists of both whole and parts. By interacting with another thing, or antithesis, a thing as a whole both remains partly the same and becomes partly different through undergoing change resulting from influences by the other thing. Each new influence on a developing thing becomes a new part of it, and each such part also remains partly the same as it was before it influenced the developing thing and becomes partly different by doing so. Every synthesis resulting from the joining of two things, or theses, is a new whole, in which the two things, although wholes in other ways, function as its parts.

WHOLENESS INVOLVES DIALECTIC. A whole and its parts are different. A whole and a part exist as antitheses. But neither can continue to exist without continuing interdependence and interaction with each other. As both continue temporally, each continues to be partly the same and partly different as a result of such continuing interaction. But a whole continues to interact dialectically with all of its parts; and all of the parts interdepend and interact, even if not directly, with each other dialectically. By continuing to function together, a whole and its opposing parts constitute an organic whole, a synthesis of whole and parts, that also functions as a new thesis in interaction with other organic wholes.

PARTIALITY INVOLVES DIALECTIC. For each part of a whole has its interrelations with the whole as fundamental parts of itself. Any change in the whole thereby produces a change in it. So changed, it may be mostly the same yet also somewhat different than before. The part as the same and the part as different function as antitheses, that is, antithetical aspects of the part as a continuing synthesis of both such sameness and difference.

Events and Duration

DIALECTIC INVOLVES BOTH EVENTS AND DURATIONS. It does so not merely because these involve each other, but because dialectic is processual and involves both persistence and multiplicities of changes. Each interaction between a thesis and an antithesis is an event, if not a series of events, each of which endures long enough for it to occur. But also each of the antitheses continues to endure while such interaction occurs, thereby remaining the same, and changes by incorporating within itself the results of such interaction, thereby becoming different; it is thus a synthesis of such sameness and difference.

If the two antitheses, by mutually sustaining stable interactions with each other, thereby produce a new synthesis, each interaction is an event in a series of events producing the stability and sustaining the synthesis as a new thesis. Several kinds of duration are involved, namely, that within each event, that within the series of events, that within each of the antitheses while it participates in and sustains the synthesis, and that of the synthesis as long as it continues (to say nothing, for example, of durations involved within the parts of each of the antitheses and in the relations of the synthesis as a thesis to other coordinate theses).

EVENTS INVOLVE DIALECTIC. Each event involves, minimally, one change. To change is to become different. A thing that changes is the same thing before and after the change. Before the change, that difference which will become is not a part of the thing (thesis) and thus is opposed to it as antithesis. After the change, the thing (thesis) that changed by becoming different (incorporating an antithesis) is thus also a synthesis of such sameness and a difference.

DURATION INVOLVES DIALECTIC. For to endure is to remain the same through change (i.e., while something becomes different). A thesis that endures by remaining the same through change, through becoming different (incorporating an antithesis), thereby functions as a synthesis of such sameness and difference.

Space

DIALECTIC INVOLVES SPACE. Space is what is between two or more coexisting things when nothing else is between them. For each thesis (existing thing), there is at least one antithesis (another coexisting thing). The external relation between some coexisting antitheses (such as I and the apple I am about to eat) is obviously spatial. The external relation between other coexisting theses (such as the one difference minimally involved in one change) is not so obvious; but whatever keeps a thesis and its antithesis from being identical involves some difference, some coexistential otherness, which functions as spatial. Although the nothing between the sameness and difference minimally involved in one change may be infinitesimal, it is not no nothing as long as each is genuinely other than the other.

Two antitheses coexisting in, and with, a synthesis involve spatial relations with that thesis (synthesis) in whatever way they both coexist with it and are other than it. The more complex the theses involved in dialectic, the more such dialectic is involved spatially.

SPACE INVOLVES DIALECTIC.   For space exists when two or more things coexist. Any two coexisting things are not each other and are thereby antithetical to each other; they thus function as antitheses. Their continuing to coexist as anthitheses involves their interacting with each other at least by not being each other at each additional common unit of time. Perpetuation of their antithetical coexistence perpetuates their spatial relatedness, and the stability generated thereby functions synthetically. Perhaps the synthetic character of space may be more obvious when several things (antitheses) coexist and share a common space (nothingness) between them, or where the space within an empty room is a nothingness that synthesizes the nothingness existing between the east–west walls, the north–south walls, and the floor and ceiling.

Relations

DIALECTIC INVOLVES RELATIONS.   It involves both the external and internal nature of relations. Two antitheses as opposed to each other are externally related, but as sharing something in common with respect to which they are opposed, they are internally related. A synthesis of two antitheses is internally related to both because both are ingredient in it, and it has become ingredient in them; yet as a new and different thesis it is also opposed to them and externally related to them. Each thesis, as it grows dialectically, is first opposed and externally related to its antithesis, and then identified and internally related to that part (or, when eating an apple, all) of the antithesis it incorporates within itself as a continuing synthesis.

RELATIONS INVOLVE DIALECTIC.   Any two things that are related are externally related in being two different things and are internally related in sharing the same relation. As two and different, the things are antitheses, and, as internally related through sharing the same relation, they function synthetically. The more internally related two things are, the more synthetical they are and the more dialectical process perpetuates their "positive synthesis" (i.e., the sharing of more in common that is positive than is negative). The more externally related two things are, the more antithetical they are and the more dialectical process perpetuates their "negative synthesis" (i.e., the sharing of more in common that is negative than is positive [exemplified, perhaps, by what astronomers now call a "black hole"]). Dialecticians have been so preoccupied with theory of new wholes (positive syntheses) that they have neglected theory of new holes (negative syntheses).

Action

DIALECTIC INVOLVES ACTION.   It includes both agency and patiency. Dialectic proceeds by one thing (thesis) acting on another thing (antithesis) as a patient which in turn reacts and acts (as agent) on the one thing (now acting as patient). When a thesis incorporates into its continuing being something received (as patient) from its antithesis, it at least partly transforms what is received into being the same as itself again acting as agent. Thus both agency and patiency are inherent in dialectical process.

When two antitheses, by virtue of their continuing interaction (as both agents and patients), establish a new thesis synthetically, the new thesis as product of their joint action functions as a patient, for its very being and nature was received from them; but it, in turn, as a thesis acts both as an agent in its interrelations with other coordinate theses and as an extension of the agencies of the antitheses on which it continues to depend. But the two antitheses, because receiving the services of the synthesis in extending their agency, function also as patients.

ACTION INVOLVES DIALECTIC. Each existing thing exists in the presence of other things, and its own act of being in such a presence also enacts its relations, negative and positive, to such other beings. It acts as a thesis which, by enacting a relation to another thing, generates the functioning of that thing as an antithesis. If the action continues, as it does if the things continue to exist, the other thing reacts as antithesis, either as a reagent or if inert (i.e., incapable of reacting), then somehow merely as patient. If antithetical action continues, synthesis develops. If the antithetical thing ceases, then a dialectic of cessation is involved.

Patience also involves dialectic. For to act as patient is to be the recipient of previous action, and to react is to have an antithesis already in action.

Purpose

DIALECTIC IS PURPOSIVE. It is purposive in the sense that it always has direction, even multiple direction, inherent in its processes. When a thesis becomes related to an antithesis, the becoming of that relation involves an aim and a goal, for the direction of the relation from the thesis to the antithesis involves aiming and the resulting functioning of the other thing as antithesis involves it, thus functioning as a goal even when such relating seems instantaneous. When two antitheses join in supporting a synthesis, they must aim at it as goal. But also as such synthetic support continues, each (thesis, antithesis, synthesis) continues to serve the others with purpose (aim and goal) involved in each interaction between them. When I eat an apple, my purposes are served, but some of those of the apple's nature cease; however, by serving my purposes, the apple generates in me an aim to perpetuate apple species through replanting apple trees, thereby achieving a complex of goals.

PURPOSE INVOLVES DIALECTIC. For any sense in which aim and goal as opposites are antitheses involves a dialectical interaction between them needed for the emergence of purpose as their synthesis. Without both goal as antithesis and purpose as synthesis, an aim cannot realize its nature.

Causation

DIALECTIC INVOLVES CAUSATION. This is so not merely because, according to the present hypothesis, causation is a category of existence, but because dialectic itself, so to speak, involves the causing of effects. Whenever any thesis acts so as to treat another thesis as an antithesis, that other thing is influenced causally to the extent that such antithetical character becomes a part of its nature. If it reacts and interacts with the first thesis so as to produce a synthesis, such a synthesis is an effect of their interaction. Such a synthesis functioning as a new thesis interacting with other theses extends the causal effectiveness of the first two theses indirectly through it. If I cannot survive without eating, then the dialectical process involved in my incorporating the apple as antithesis into my body as synthesis is essential in causing my survival.

CAUSATION INVOLVES DIALECTIC. For cause and effect as polar

opposites are antitheses, and each depends on the other for its being and nature. Causation as synthesis of cause and effect can continue only through dialectical recurrence of thing as effect being transformed into thing as cause of other effects, and so on. Causation, as we have seen, is very complex; the ways in which dialectic is involved in each of its complexities are a subject for another study.

37 / THREE KINDS OF DIALECTIC

The foregoing treatment has been limited largely to synthetic dialectic, the only kind traditionally recognized. My own studies have uncovered both analytic dialectic and the joint operation of analytic and synthetic dialectic in what I call *organitic dialectic*.

Synthetic Dialectic

Although synthetic dialectic is of many different kinds, as we have already indicated, common to all such kinds is a distinction between two or more theses functioning as antitheses with their joint and cooperative functioning in supporting another thesis called a "synthesis." Each synthesis functions as a whole, because it involves two or more antitheses as parts. So synthetic dialectic always involves a parts–whole situation in which the whole depends on the parts. If the synthesis emerges processually, then the synthesis arises as a "new thesis," and the "new whole" is made up of the antitheses as parts.

Analytic Dialectic

When a fertilized ovum exists as a single cell, it can continue to live, apparently, only by a process in which it divides itself into two cells (two antitheses), then four, then eight, and so on, while at the same time retaining a wholeness that enables it to continue to act in ways that coordinate the functionings of the cells as a body, later able to play football, for example. When we imagine a living body as a synthesis of its cells and organs, we forget that the original cell had a unity and wholeness about it which was not totally destroyed by its division into many cells, because the division was organic and not complete. The emergence of each cell occurred within a larger whole of which it became a new part. If the process of creating new wholes from preexisting parts is called "synthetic," then the process of creating new parts from pre-existing wholes is properly called "analytic." If the new synthetic whole is a "synthesis," then the new analytic part (which also functions as a whole of its own parts) may be called an "analythesis."

Just as some synthetic processes involve the destruction of one or more of the antitheses, as when I survive by eating an apple, so some analytic processes involve the separation of analytheses from the wholes in which they originate. When I bleed, the cells which originated in me cease to be a part of me. And when I leave home, I tend to become a thing separated at least somewhat from the family within which I was socially nurtured. Some separated analytheses are thereby destroyed (as when my blood cells die) and some become new theses and participate in new syntheses (as a sperm cell originating in my body fertilizes an ovum and produces a child, or my leaving home to marry produces a new family).

Organitic Dialectic

The joint operation of synthetic and analytic dialectic may be observed in our previous example of a fertilized ovum dividing itself. Normally isolated ova and sperm can neither produce offspring nor survive very long. Their synthesis in a fertilized ovum is necessary for their continuance. And the continuance of their synthesis apparently depends on its subsequent divisions, in which

chromosome pairs analogous to those in the original synthesis recur in each subdivided cell. Dialectic is "more organitic" when
there is more rather than less interaction between the analytic
and synthetic aspects of a complex dialectical process.

Deeper analysis of synthetic dialectic reveals analytic aspects
already present, for usually only a part of each antithesis functions
in a synthesis; so any differentiation of such a part in an antithesis involves it in functioning already as an analythesis. And
analytic dialectic involves some contribution from each of several
parts within the whole (as well as from the whole as a whole) in
the production of a new part.

Popular interest in dialectic is lacking, I suspect, not because it
is unimportant, but because the intricacies almost immediately
obvious tend to baffle minds which somehow seem to get along
with simpler modes of understanding.[1]

38 / HEGEL AND MARX

The history of meanings of, and theories of, dialectic, from dialogue to category of existence is long and interesting.[1] Space remains for mentioning only the two most well-known types, those attributed to Hegel and Marx.

Hegel

Georg Wilhelm Friedrich Hegel was an Absolute Idealist who saw the whole universe as a dynamic process in which thought and being are identical and rational, such that one thing necessarily results from another and such that not only are all opposites (contradictories) *aufgehoben* (i.e., gathered up and preserved in their syntheses) but that the higher stages are already implicit in the lower.

If we look for the lowest or first stage, the beginning, we find first that "there is Nothing: Something is to become. The Beginning is not pure Nothing, but a Nothing from which Something is to proceed; so that Being is already contained in the Beginning. The Beginning thus contains both, Being and Nothing; it is the unity of Being and Nothing, or is Not-being which is Being, and Being which is also Not-being."[2] So even in the beginning we find a synthesis of two antitheses, being and not-being or something and nothing.

At the highest level, The Absolute, we find a synthesis of everything, which includes all negation as well as all affirmation, all that is in any way and all that is not, including the ways in which each thing is not every other thing. In such final synthesis, the absoluteness of each particular as a thing in itself and as opposed to other things is also retained; otherwise something would be missing from that which includes everything.

Marx

Karl Marx, who studied Hegelian philosophy in the University of Berlin soon after Hegel died, preferred Historical Materialism in which the play of forces, exemplified in the struggle of economic classes for supremacy (rather than in an eternal rational order fulfilling itself in history), played the primary determining role in metaphysical as well as political developments. It is said that Marx turned Hegel upside down, transforming the dialectic of history from idealism to materialism.

However, since Marx regarded the overthrow of the capitalist class by the laboring class and the emergence of a classless society as inevitable, something of the logical necessity inherent in Hegelian ideals of rationality seems to have been retained in his view. Also, instead of the antitheses, capitalism and proletarianism, being *aufgehoben* (i.e., gathered up and preserved), both are to be destroyed. Whereas Hegel eulogized the German state as a pinnacle of political development, Marx idealized a withering away of the state, which he regarded as an instrument of oppression.

Despite the tremendous political influence of Marx and his fellows (Feuerbach, Engels, Lenin), detailed analysis of dialectic as a logical and metaphysical process seems missing in their theories. Although opposed to that kind of materialism which treats things atomistically, Marx advocated the use of scientific methods which left issues regarding the nature of science and the role of dialectic in it that continue to be debated by his followers.

NOTES

Notes to Chapter 7: Differences

1. W. T. Stace, *The Theory of Knowledge and Existence* (Oxford: Clarendon, 1932), p. 304.
2. F. H. Bradley, *Appearance and Reality* (London: Oxford University Press, 1930), p. 107.
3. Charles S. Pierce, *Collected Works* (Cambridge, Mass.: Harvard University Press, 1960), 1:566.
4. S. C. Chatterjee and D. M. Datta, *An Introduction to Indian Philosophy*, 5th ed. (Calcutta: University of Calcutta, 1954), p. 427.
5. Plotinus *Ennead* 5. 9. 10 in Joseph Katz, tr., *The Philosophy of Plotinus* (New York: Appleton, 1950), p. 38.
6. James M. Baldwin, *Dictionary of Philosophy and Psychology* (New York: Macmillan, 1911), 1:506.
7. Mohan Lal Mehta, *Outlines of Jaina Philosophy* (Bangalore: Jain Mission Society, 1954), p. 25.
8. Samuel Alexander, *Space, Time, and Deity* (London: Macmillan, 1920, 1927), 1:197, 198.

Notes to Chapter 8: Change

1. Charles M. Bakewell, *Sourcebook in Ancient Philosophy* (New York: Scribner, 1907), p. 33.
2. Cf. Jadunath Sinha, *History of Indian Philosophy* (Calcutta: Central Book Agency, 1952), pp. 284–286.
3. See Bakewell, op. cit., pp. 13–17.

4. He argued against the possibility of motion through a space made up of points by supposing that an arrow in any given moment in its flight must be at rest in some particular point. See ibid., p. 24.

5. Sinha, op. cit., p. 501.

6. S. Radhakrishnan, *Indian Philosophy* (London: Allen and Unwin, 1923, 1948), 2:532.

7. Arthur Avalon, tr., *The Greatness of Shiva* (Madras: Ganesh, 1916, 1953), pp. 6–7.

8. A. E. Taylor, *Elements of Metaphysics* (London: Methuen, 1903, 1924), p. 161.

9. Ibid., p. 159.

10. W. D. Ross, tr., *The Works of Aristotle Translated into English* (Oxford: Clarendon, 1928), vol. 8, *Metaphysica* 1073a23–27.

11. Plotinus *Ennead* 2. 5. 5 in Joseph Katz, tr., *The Philosophy of Plotinus* (New York: Appleton, 1950), p. 133.

12. Henri Bergson, *Creative Evolution* (New York: Holt, Rinehart and Winston, 1911, 1944), pp. 4, 374.

13. Henri Bergson, *An Introduction to Metaphysics* (New York: Putnam, 1912), pp. 65, 67–68.

14. Chen Li-fu, *Philosophy of Life* (New York: Philosophical Library, 1948), p. 25.

15. Lawrence Hyde, *I Who Am* (Reigate, Surrey: Omega Press, 1954), p. 96.

16. Harilal Jain, "Jainism: Its Philosophy and Ethics," in *The Cultural Heritage of India* (Calcutta: Ramakrishna Mission Institute of Culture, 1937, 1958), 1:420.

Notes to Chapter 9: Substance

1. W. D. Ross, tr., *The Works of Aristotle Translated into English* (Oxford: Clarendon, 1928), vol. 1, *Categoriae* 5. 4b17ff.

2. Ibid., 5. 3b33.

3. Ibid., 5. 3b25.

4. Ibid., 5. 3b10.

5. See Ross, op. cit., vol. 8, Z. 13. 25.

6. Cf. John Locke, *An Essay concerning Human Understanding* (London: Basham Churchill, 1690, 1696), book 2, chap. 23.

7. See Ross, op. cit., vol. 8, Z. 1 34–35.

8. Cf. Benedict Spinoza, *Ethics*, tr. William Hale White (New York: Macmillan, 1883), Proposition 14.

Notes to Chapter 10: Wholes

1. P. T. Raju, *Idealistic Thought of India* (London: Allen and Unwin, 1953), p. 437.

2. For further exploration of issues, see "Wholes, Sums, and Organic Unities" by Ernest Nagel in his *The Structure of Science* (New York: Harcourt Brace Jovanovich, 1961), pp. 380–397.

3. Raju, op. cit., p. 483.

4. Ibid.

5. Elmer O'Brien, tr., *The Essential Plotinus* (New York: New American Library, 1964), p. 80.

6. Lawrence Hyde, *I Who Am* (Reigate, Surrey: Omega Press, 1954), p. 138.

7. William James, *Some Problems of Philosophy* (London: Longmans, Green, 1911), p. 136.

8. Max Wertheimer, in *A Sourcebook of Gestalt Psychology*, ed. William D. Ellis (London: Routledge & Kegan Paul, 1938), p. 2.

9. Robert Latta, *Leibniz, The Monadology* (Oxford: Oxford University Press, 1898), p. 31.

10. S. Radhakrishnan, *Indian Philosophy* (London: Allen and Unwin, 1923, 1948), 2:537.

11. Ibid., p. 536.

12. John Wild, *Spinoza, Selections* (New York: Scribner, 1930), p. 36.

13. Latta, op. cit., p. 23.

Notes to Chapter 11: Time

1. Roy Wood Sellars, *The Philosophy of Physical Realism* (New York: Macmillan, 1932), p. 307.
2. Archie J. Bahm, *Philosophy: An Introduction* (New York: Wiley, 1953), p. 247.
3. See chapter 10.
4. Jadunath Sinha, *History of Indian Philosophy* (Calcutta: Central Book Agency, 1952), 2:541.
5. See H. G. Alexander, ed., *The Leibniz-Clarke Correspondence* (Manchester: Manchester University Press, 1956), third and fifth papers.
6. Isaac Newton, *Principia*, scholium.
7. Sinha, op. cit., pp. 50 ff.
8. Cf. P. T. Raju, *The Philosophical Traditions of India* (Pittsburgh: University of Pittsburgh Press, 1971), pp. 128–129.

Notes to Chapter 12: Space

1. Paul Weiss, *Reality* (New York: Peter Smith, 1949), p. 185.
2. "Sometimes it would seem as if the whole earth counted as a point." Bertrand Russell, *The Analysis of Matter* (London: K. Paul, Trench, Trubner, 1921), p. 57.
3. *Seventh New Intercollegiate Dictionary* (Springfield, Ill.: Merriam, 1965).
4. Cf. Charles M. Bakewell, *Sourcebook in Ancient Philosophy* (New York: Scribner, 1907), pp. 13, 17.
5. Isaac Newton, *Principia*, scholium 2.
6. René Descartes, *Principles of Philosophy*, part 2, section 10, in Elisabeth Anscombe and Peter Thomas Geach, trs., *Descartes' Philosophical Writings* (London: Nelson, 1959).
7. H. G. Alexander, ed., *The Leibniz-Clarke Correspondence* (Manchester: Manchester University Press, 1956), sections 4, 33, 54.

8. Francis Herbert Bradley, *Appearance and Reality* (Oxford: Clarendon, 1893, 1930), p. 31.
9. Ibid., p. 32.
10. Cf. ibid., pp. 181–196.
11. Jadunath Sinha, *History of Indian Philosophy* (Calcutta: Central Book Agency, 1952), 2:541.
12. Norman Kemp Smith, tr., *Immanuel Kant's Critique of Pure Reason* (London: Macmillan, 1929), p. 71.
13. Samuel Alexander, *Space, Time, and Deity* (London: Macmillan, 1920, 1927), 1:vi, 48.

Notes to Chapter 13: Relations

1. Otis Lee, *Existence and Inquiry* (Chicago: University of Chicago Press, 1949), p. 119.
2. Hubert G. Alexander, "Concerning a Postulate of Fitness," *Philosophy and Phenomenological Research* 14 (March 1954): 309.
3. Lee, op. cit., p. 119.
4. P. T. Raju, *Thought and Reality* (London: Allen and Unwin, 1937), p. 48.
5. Roy Wood Sellars, *Evolutionary Naturalism* (Chicago: Open Court, 1922), p. 215.
6. Francis Herbert Bradley, *Appearance and Reality* (Oxford: Clarendon, 1893, 1930), p. 392.
7. D. W. Gotshalk, *Structure and Reality* (New York: Dial, 1937), p. 77.
8. Sellars, op. cit., p. 198.
9. Ibid., p. 207.

Notes to Chapter 14: Universals

1. Roy Wood Sellars, *The Philosophy of Physical Realism* (New York: Macmillan, 1932), p. 161.

2. Cf. B. Jowett, *The Dialogues of Plato* (London: Oxford University Press, 1892), 3:447 ff.

3. Cf. Wilhelm Windelband, *History of Philosophy*, 2nd ed., rev. and enl. (London: Macmillan, 1893, 1901), pp. 287–299, 337–345.

4. Cf. Jowett, op. cit.

5. Thomas Aquinas, *Concerning Being and Essence*, tr. George G. Leckie (New York: Appleton, 1937), p. 5.

6. David Hume, *A Treatise of Human Nature*, ed. L. A. Selby-Bigge (Oxford: Clarendon, 1896), book 1, part 1, section 1.

7. Ibid., part 2, section 2.

8. John Dewey, *Experience and Nature*, 2nd ed. (Chicago: Open Court, 1925, 1929), p. 117.

9. Henri Bergson, *An Introduction to Metaphysics*, tr. T. E. Hulme (New York: Putnam, 1912), p. 76.

10. Jean-Paul Sartre, *Existentialism and Human Emotions* (New York: Philosophical Library, 1957), p. 15.

11. Norman Kemp Smith, tr. *Immanuel Kant's Critique of Pure Reason* (London: Macmillan, 1929), p. 93.

12. George Santayana, *The Realms of Being* (New York: Scribner, 1940, 1942).

13. Ibid., pp. 18, 19, 189, 202.

14. Bertrand Russell, "On the Relations of Universals and Particulars," *Proceedings of the Aristotelian Society* 12 (1911–1912). Quoted in *The Problem of Universals*, ed. Charles Landesman (New York: Basic Books, 1971), pp. 21, 35.

15. Alfred North Whitehead, *Process and Reality* (New York: Macmillan, 1929), p. 239.

16. Ibid., p. 76.

17. Cf. Swami Nikhilananda, *The Upanishads* (New York: Harper, 1949), 1:25–106; Kenneth K. Inada, *Nagarjuna: A Translation of His Mulamadhyamikakarika* (Tokyo: Hokuseido Press, 1970); Bukkhu J. Kashyap, *The Abhidhamma Philosophy* (Nalanda, Buddha Vihara, 1942, 1954), vol. 1.

Notes to Chapter 15: Action

1. Robert F. Spencer, "The Nature and Value of Functionalism in Anthropology," in *Functionalism in the Social Sciences*, monograph 5 (Philadelphia: American Academy of Political and Social Science, 1965), p. 13.
2. Thomas Aquinas, *The Summa Contra Gentiles of Saint Thomas Aquinas* (London: Burne, Oates & Washburne, 1923), 3:1:8.
3. Borden Parker Bowne, *Metaphysics, A Study of First Principles* (New York: Harper, 1882), pp. 55–56.
4. Malcolm Knox, *Action* (London: Allen and Unwin, 1968), p. 83.

Notes to Chapter 16: Purpose

1. Francis S. Hasserot, *Essays in the Logic of Being* (New York: Macmillan, 1932), p. 284.
2. Plotinus *Ennead* 5 in Joseph Katz, tr., *The Philosophy of Plotinus* (New York: Appleton, 1950), p. 14.
3. Hasserot, op. cit., p. 282.
4. A. E. Taylor, *Elements of Metaphysics* (London: Methuen, 1903, 1924), p. 158.
5. Hasserot, op. cit., p. 281.
6. Ibid., p. 305.
7. See footnote 5.

Notes to Chapter 17: Intelligence

1. See A. J. Bahm, "Meanings of Intelligence," *Philosophical Studies* 14 (1965): 151–155.
2. See A. J. Bahm, ed., *Tao Teh King by Lao Tzu, Interpreted as Nature and Intelligence* (New York: Frederick Ungar, 1958), pp. 23, 26.

3. Ibid., p. 52.
4. See A. J. Bahm, *The Heart of Confucius* (Tokyo: John Weatherhill; New York: Walker, 1969), p. 129.
5. Ibid., p. 130.
6. George Herbert Mead, *The Philosophy of the Present*, ed. Arthur E. Murphy (Chicago: Open Court, 1932), p. 4.
7. S. Radhakrishnan, *Indian Philosophy* (London: Allen and Unwin, 1923, 1948), 2:483.

Notes to Chapter 18: Process

1. (New York: Random House, 1965).
2. A quarterly begun in 1971.

Notes to Chapter 19: Cause and Effect

1. D. W. Gotshalk, *Structure and Reality* (New York: Dial, 1937), p. 136.
2. T. M. P. Mahadevan, *A Study in Early Advaita* (Madras: University of Madras, 1952), p. 134.
3. S. Radhakrishnan, *Indian Philosophy* (London: Allen and Unwin, 1923, 1948), 2:758.
4. Herbert V. Guenther, *Yuganaddha, The Tantric View of Life* (Banaras: Chowkhambra Sanskrit Series Office, 1952), p. 146.
5. Radhakrishnan, op. cit., p. 256.
6. M. Hiriyanna, *The Essentials of Indian Philosophy* (New York: Macmillan, 1949), p. 109.
7. A. J. Bahm, "Emergence of Purpose," *Journal of Philosophy* 44 (Nov. 6, 1947): 633.
8. D. W. Gotshalk, "Causality as an Ontological Relation," *Monist* 40 (April 1930): 244.
9. Gotshalk, *Structure and Reality*, p. 183.
10. (London: Williams and Norgate, 1923).
11. For details, see my *Philosophy: An Introduction* (New York: Wiley, 1953), chap. 18.
12. Radhakrishnan, op. cit., p. 94.

Note to Chapter 21: Cause and Other Conditions

1. Cf. W. D. Ross, tr., *The Works of Aristotle Translated into English* (Oxford: Clarendon, 1928), vol. 8, *Metaphysica* 983a.

Notes to Chapter 22: Cause and Direction

1. D. W. Gotshalk, *Structure and Reality* (New York: Dial, 1937), p. 163.
2. David Hume, *A Treatise of Human Nature*, ed. L. A. Selby-Bigge (Oxford: Clarendon, 1896), part 3, section 2.
3. Ibid.

Notes to Chapter 23: Cause and Time

1. Roy Wood Sellars, *The Philosophy of Physical Realism* (New York: Macmillan, 1932), p. 358.
2. Abner Shimony, "An Ontological Examination of Causation," *Review of Metaphysics* 1 (Fall 1947): 58.

Notes to Chapter 25: Levels of Causation

1. (Springfield: Charles C Thomas, 1970).
2. See my *Philosophy: An Introduction* (New York: Wiley, 1953), chaps. 17–19.

Notes to Chapter 26: Causation and Creation

1. See *Philosophy: An Introduction*, chap. 18.
2. C. Lloyd Morgan, *Emergent Evolution* (London: Williams and Norgate, 1923), p. 3.
3. *Philosophy: An Introduction*, p. 246.
4. See "Creativity through Interdependence," *Personalist* 49 (Autumn 1968): 523–530.

Note to Chapter 28: Causation and Destruction

1. See my *Polarity, Dialectic, and Organicity* (Springfield: Charles C Thomas, 1970), chaps. 13, 14.

Note to Chapter 29: Final Causation

1. See further, "Emergence of Values," *Journal of Philosophy* 45 (July 15, 1948): 411–414.

Notes to Chapter 32: Causation and Potentiality

1. W. D. Ross, tr. *The Works of Aristotle Translated into English* (Oxford: Clarendon, 1928), vol. 8, *Metaphysica* 1049b5.
2. Paul Weiss, "On the Difference between Actuality and Possibility," *Review of Metaphysics* 10 (September 1956): 165.
3. Aristotle, in W. D. Ross, op. cit., 1047b5.
4. Ibid., 1048b5.

Notes to Chapter 35: Ingredients in Dialectic

1. Explored in my *Polarity, Dialectic, and Organicity* (Springfield: Charles C Thomas, 1970), chap. 16.
2. See ibid., chaps. 6, 11, 16.
3. For a much more detailed analysis of the ingredients in dialectic, see ibid., chaps. 1–20.

Note to Chapter 37: Three Kinds of Dialectic

1. For separate chapters summarizing the intricacies of analytic and organitic dialectic, see ibid., chaps. 16, 17.

Notes to Chapter 38: Hegel and Marx

1. See "Dialectic," *Encylopedia of Philosophy* (New York: Macmillan and Free Press, 1967), 2:385–389.
2. W. H. Johnston and L. G. Struthers, tr., *Hegel's Science of Logic* (New York: Macmillan, 1929), 1:85.

GLOSSARY

Absolute Idealist A philosopher who holds that the entire universe is mental in nature or that the universe is a mind. Hegel called such universe "The Absolute" and regarded its operation as a rational, dialectical, concrete, historical process.

Advaita Vedanta Nondualistic Vedantism. Indian philosophy that regards itself as the end or culmination of the development of Vedic philosophy. Holds that ultimate reality, *Nirguna Brahman*, pure indistinct being (*sat*), awareness (*chit*), and bliss (*ananda*), is indistinct from (nondifferent from) *Saguna Brahman*, or *maya* (illusion), the rest of the pluralistic(dynamic, divine, living, disturbed, conscious and unconscious universe.

Alexander, Hubert G(riggs) (1909–) Professor of Philosophy, University of New Mexico, specializing in philosophy of language. Works: *Time as Dimension and History*, 1945; *Language and Thinking*, 1967.

Alexander, Samuel (1859–1938) British philosopher noted as an emergent evolutionist. He conceived existence as based in a dynamic, four-dimensional space-time, emerging through levels of matter, life, mind, and God, each higher level depending on the lower but also influencing its behavior and subsequent development. Chief work: *Space, Time, and Deity*, two vols., 1920.

Aquinas, Thomas (1225–1274) Dominican philosopher who modified the doctrines of Augustine, who had been much influenced by Plato. Aquinas incorporated many ideas derived from Aristotle which were made available to him by Arabic scholars. His highly rationalistic synthesis of theological and other metaphysical ideas have been most influential in shaping the philosophies not only of orthodox Roman Catholics but of

243

many unorthodox thinkers of the Western world. Chief works: *Summa Contra Gentiles*, c. 1260; *Summa Theologica*, 1265–1272.

Aristotle (384–322 B.C.) Greek philosopher, student and critic of Plato. Except for Plato probably the most influential single philosopher in Western civilization. Author of more than twenty works. See W. D. Ross, *The Works of Aristotle Translated into English*, 1920–1925.

Avidya Sanskrit word meaning inability to see clearly or tendency not to see what really is.

Bergson, Henri (1859–1941) French philosopher who stressed intuitive awareness of the flux of experience as grasping ultimate reality—a vital urge that intellectual knowledge tries to capture in fixed concepts and static structures. English translations of his works include: *Time and Free Will*, 1910; *Creative Evolution*, 1911; *Matter and Memory*, 1911; *An Introduction to Metaphysics*, 1912; *Two Sources of Religion and Morality*, 1935.

Bhavanga Pali term meaning tendency to continue, used by Theravada Buddhists to refer to ultimate reality as a perfectly quiescent flow of being.

Bradley, Francis Herbert (1846–1924) British Absolute Idealist who advocated a coherence theory of the nature of truth and criticized doctrines involving ideas of external relations. Chief work: *Appearance and Reality*, 1893.

Democritus (c. 460–360 B.C.) Early Greek materialist who proposed that everything is composed of hard uncuttable (hence "atomic") particles falling in infinite space, which have sharp, smooth, or hooked surfaces causing them to associate in different compounds.

Descartes, René (1596–1650) French Roman Catholic who, dissatisfied with lack of agreement among philosophers, decided to rethink with certainty rational arguments for the existence of self, the physical world, and God. His metaphysical theory is called "dualism" because he claimed that the world, including persons, is made up of two kinds of substance, minds or spirits and bodies or matter, which are entirely different in nature. Each has a basic attribute: mind thinks, matter extends. However, God, the creating substance, involves more than both mind and matter as created substances. Chief work: *Discourse on Method* (several translations).

Dewey, John (1859–1952) American pragmatist who saw scientific methods of problem solving as intelligent extensions of Darwinian struggle-for-existence and survival-of-the-fit biological evolutionary processes. Reconstructing traditional philosophical problems from this perspective, he saw persons and their environments interacting in ways that influence (i.e., causally modify) each other. The actual world is genuinely different as a result of problem solving, and when successful problem solvers survive, their ideas survive with them. When similar problems recur, they try out the same methods which, if repeated successfully, become habits. Institutions are social habits that should be retained as long as they serve efficiently and discarded or reorganized when failing to do so. Works include: *How We Think*, 1910; *Reconstruction in Philosophy*, 1920; *Experience and Nature*, 1933; *Logic, The Theory of Inquiry*, 1939.

Eleatics Early Greek thinkers who lived in Elea, in southern Italy, argued that absolute change is impossible and unthinkable and that by nature things are permanent. They include: Xenophanes (570–480 B.C.), Parmenides (fifth century B.C.), and Zeno (490–430 B.C.).

Élan vital Vital urge, or tendency of life to go on. A word used by Bergson to name the will to live expressed as the forward flow of experience.

Emergentists C. Lloyd Morgan, Samuel Alexander, Roy Wood Sellars, Jan Christian Smuts, and others who hold that existence evolves in such a way that, from time to time, some genuinely new kinds of organizations of things become stabilized as new kinds and new levels of being. Although unpredictable, even in principle, by complete knowledge of a lower level, each new higher level evolves its own structures, substances, qualities, centers of causation, and laws of behavior. Higher-level beings may cease to exist, but their nature cannot be explained by reducing it to the natures of the more elementary organisms upon which it depends.

Gotshalk, D(illman) W(alter) (1901–1973) Professor Emeritus, University of Illinois, reconstructed metaphysics on a "structure principle," following two previous modern epochs that emphasized the "substance principle" and then the "evolution principle." Metaphysical works: *Structure and Reality*, 1937; *Metaphysics in Modern Times*, 1940.

Gunas Sanskrit word meaning either qualities (distinctions) or tendencies (forces). *Nirguna Brahman* is without qualities or tendencies. "The three *gunas*" (*rajas*, the tendency to excite, arouse, activate; *sattwa*, the tendency to persevere, to remain quiescent, to retain calm amid tensions or disturbances; and *tamas*, the tendency to be lax, to degenerate, to wither away without fulfillment) exist in all things, plants, men, nations, deities; and when one dominates, the thing behaves accordingly. Yogic practice aims, with the aid of *sattwa*, to keep all three in quiescent equilibrium.

Hegel, Georg Wilhelm Friedrich (1770–1831) German Absolute Idealist who helped to revolutionize philosophizing by interpreting thought as not merely abstract but also as concrete, that is, as part of an historical process that proceeds dialectically. English translations of his works include: *Phenomenology of Mind*, two vols., 1910; *Science of Logic*, two vols., 1929.

Hume, David (1711–1776) Scottish agnostic who, accepting the empiricist doctrine that knowledge originates in sensory experience, concluded that certainty about metaphysical principles, especially causation, is impossible. Works include: *A Treatise of Human Nature*, 1739–1740; *Enquiry concerning the Human Understanding*, 1748.

Jainism Indian philosophical and religious movement that claims to have originated before the Vedas. Holds that souls are eternal, thus uncreated, are perpetually reincarnated in accordance with the law of *karma*, and must work their own way, unaided, to the goal of life, a heavenly, omniscient condition completely freed from desire.

James, William (1842–1910) American pragmatist famous for interpreting true ideas as those that "work" or bring us satisfactorily to the solutions of our problems. He refuted Hume's agnosticism by demonstrating that satisfaction is all that we require of beliefs in the first place. He favored a pluralistic universe. Works include: *The Will to Believe*, 1897; *Pragmatism*, 1907; *A Pluralistic Universe*, 1909.

Kant, Immanuel (1724–1804) German rationalist, influenced by Hume's agnosticism, restored confidence in metaphysics as a science of phenomenal (apparent) experience by showing how categories employed in interpreting experience are necessary forms of intuition or concepts of understanding supplied by the mind. He continued to be agnostic about the nature of real things or "things-in-themselves." English translations: *Critique of Judgment*, 1892, 1914; *Critique of Pure Reason*, 1929; *Critique of Practical Reason*, 1949.

Karma Sanskrit word meaning action or work where effects are intended. Presupposed is a pervasive principle of reciprocity, spoken of as "the law of *karma*," according to which goods one intends will be returned, and evils one intends will be returned, if not immediately, then later, even determining conditions in a next life.

Lao-tzu (c. 570–? B. C.) Reputed author of the *Tao Te Ching* (Book of Nature and Intelligence) expounding a simple, common-sense view of nature and human nature that has persisted as a dominant philosophical tradition through Chinese history.

Leibniz, Gottfried Wilhelm (1646–1716) German philosopher who sought to unify philosophy by seeking a common language or "universal calculus" on which all could agree. His metaphysics pictured minds ("monads") as mirroring the whole world, even if very unclearly, and as being spiritual in inner nature even though appearing as material in nature from their exteriors. An extreme rationalist who believed that God, omniscient (i.e., knowing all the possible universes which could be created) and omnibenevolent (i.e., wanting what is best), therefore created this one, the best of all possible worlds. English translation of chief work: *The Monadology*, 1898.

Libido Word used by Sigmund Freud (1856–1939), father of psychoanalysis, to name the tendency of living force to assert itself. It appears as desire, will, motivation, including sexual drive. Its restriction, repression, or redirection beget certain results naturally which manifest themselves in neuroses and psychoses.

Locke, John (1632–1714) British empiricist who denied the existence of innate ideas and conceived mind as a storehouse of ideas furnished by sensory experiences. He remained a realist in his theory of knowledge but critically reexamined traditional metaphysical notions and interpreted some of them as results of workings of the mind. Chief work: *An Essay on Human Understanding*, 1690.

Marx, Karl (1818–1883) German political economist who, after studying the philosophy of Hegel, developed his own Dialectical Materialism in which historical processes are claimed to evolve dialectically. Chief work: *Das Capital*, three vols., 1867, 1885, 1894.

Maya Illusion. Sanskrit word used especially by Vedantists to describe the temporal and visible world and self-ideas as distinguished from *Nirguna Brahman*, the ultimate reality which is timeless, invisible, and without self-awareness. Yet such "illusion" is powerful in the sense that all of the forces of nature, such as hurricanes and earthquakes, and life and death and wars are all parts of it.

Mead, George Herbert (1863–1931) University of Chicago philosopher and social psychologist who demonstrated social origins of self-ideas which then continue to function pragmatically (i.e., variably), depending on new kinds of situations in which a person functions and becomes aware of himself as so functioning. Works: *Philosophy of the Present*, 1932; *Mind, Self, and Society*, 1934; *Philosophy of the Act*, 1938.

Morgan, C(onway) Lloyd (1852–1936) British emergentist who clarified the doctrine by distinguishing between "resultants" (i.e., predictable outcomes of physical causal processes) and "emergents" (i.e., genuinely novel, and thereby unpredictable, organizations of being with their own novel ways of causing). Chief work: *Emergent Evolution*, 1923.

Nagarjuna (c. second century A.D.) Indian Buddhist philosopher credited with formulating the Madhyamika (Sunyavada) doctrine that ultimate reality is *sunya,* the void (i.e., void of distinctions). Chief translation: *Nagarjuna: A Translation of His Mulamadhyamakakarika,* 1970.

Newton, Isaac (1642–1727) English mathematician and philosopher whose formulation of ideas about the physical world in terms of absolute space and absolute time were most influential in early modern physics and philosophy. Work: *Mathematical Principles of Natural Philosophy,* 1687.

Nirguna Brahman Ultimate reality as conceived by Advaita Vedanta. It is Brahman without qualities, distinctions, or tendencies; yet *Saguna Brahman,* the world with qualities, distinctions and tendencies is illusory (*maya*), has no reality apart from it. *Nirguna Brahman* is (*sat*), is aware (*chit*), and is bliss (*ananda*); but these are not attributes or constituents for it is not three things but is the being of blissful awareness.

Nyaya See Nyaya-Vaisesika.

Nyaya-Vaisesika Two interrelated orthodox schools of Indian philosophy, the first concerned primarily with problems in logic and theory of knowledge, the second more with categories of existence. In contrast with Advaita Vedanta, which emphasizes unity, these schools are explicitly pluralistic.

Parmenides See Eleatics.

Peirce, Charles Sanders (1839–1914) Founder of American Pragmatism whose essays, "How to Make Our Ideas Clear" and "The Fixation of Belief," are classic statements of the pragmatic view of truth and certainty. Also a mathematician and symbolic logician. See *Collected Papers of Charles Sanders Peirce,* 1931–1935.

Plato (?427–347 B.C.) Most influential Greek philosopher. His doctrine of eternal Ideas or Forms as Archetypes after which all created things are patterned serves as a background for Western mathematics, logic, science, metaphysics, and theology. Works: *Dialogues* (several translations).

Plotinus (205–270) Neo-Platonic philosopher, influenced by Hindu thought, who conceived reality as a hierarchical scale, ranging from The One, a pure unity isolated from all else, through unity of the created (emanated) world, through levels of increasing plurality (Nous, Soul, Body) to the Void, or non-being. Chief work: *The Enneads* (several translations).

Prakriti See Sankhya-Yoga.

Purusha See Sankhya-Yoga.

Radhakrishnan, S(arvepalli) (1888–) Indian philosopher and scholar famous as a collaborator and as Vice President of India. Works include: *Indian Philosophy*, two vols., 1923, 1927; ed. of *History of Philosophy, Eastern and Western*, two vols., 1952–1953.

Raju, P(oola) T(irupati) (1904–) Indian philosopher who has taught in the United States for many years. Works: *Idealistic Thoughts of India*, 1953; *The Concept of Man*, 1960, 1966; *An Introduction to Comparative Philosophy*, 1962; *The Philosophical Traditions of India*, 1971.

Russell, Bertrand (Arthur William) (1872–1970) British philosopher, outspoken, witty, famous for having changed his views several times. Works: *The Analysis of Mind*, 1921; *The Analysis of Matter*, 1927; with A. N. Whitehead, *Principia Mathematica*, three vols., 1910–1913.

Sankhya-Yoga Two orthodox schools of Indian philosophy sharing dualistic doctrines. Two kinds of beings, *purusha* (eternal souls) and *prakriti* (nature, which, when lured by the presence of souls, devolves from a purely quiescent "unmanifest" state through consciousness (*buddhi*), self-consciousness (*ahamkara*), consciousness of desires, objects of desires, and thoughts, (*manas*, mind), the five senses, the five organs of sense, objects of sense, and subtle objects. Yogic efforts are required to master and eliminate each of these levels until the soul (pure being and awareness) is liberated from having the appearance of natural activities reflected in it. Sankhya emphasizes metaphysics. Yoga emphasizes techniques for liberation.

Santayana, George (1863–1952) Spanish-born American philosopher who, despite retaining a somewhat poetic mood, depicted the world as a complex metaphysical system with four distinguishable realms: the realm of essence, the realm of matter, the realm of spirit, and the realm of truth. Important works: *Skepticism and Animal Faith*, 1923; *The Realms of Being*, 1927–1940.

Sartre, Jean-Paul (1905–) French atheistic existentialist whose novels and dramas popularized an extreme form of Romanticism in both Europe and the United States. English translation: *Being and Nothingness*, 1956.

Sellars, Roy Wood (1880–) Chief American emergentist who remained closer to materialism than did the British emergentists. Chief works: *Critical Realism*, 1916; *Evolutionary Naturalism*, 1922; *The Philosophy of Physical Realism*, 1932.

Shankara (Samkara) (788–820) Chief formulator of Advaita Vedanta, nondualistic epitome of the Vedantic trend from pluralism to monism. Held that ultimate reality, *Nirguna Brahman*, is pure being, pure awareness, pure bliss, and that it is without distinctions, without desire, and is timeless. The apparent world, *Saguna Brahman*, has no other reality, and thus is illusory. Change in the world is caused by varying dominations by the three *gunas: rajas*, which disturbs, arouses, initiates action; *sattwa*, which stabilizes, pacifies, and quiets action; and *tamas*, which weakens, devitalizes, and thus destroys action.

Sinha, Jadunath (1892–) Sanskrit scholar and historian of Indian philosophy. Author of the most exhaustive work in its field in English. Chief work: *History of Indian Philosophy*, vol. 1, 1956, vol. 2, 1952, vol. 3, 1970.

Smuts, Jan Christian (1870–1950) South African general and prime minister who, independently, developed an emergentistic philosophy. Chief work: *Holism and Evolution*, 1926.

Spinoza, Benedict (1632–1677) Dutch Jew, expelled from his synagogue on charges of atheism and later described as a "God-intoxicated man." Sought to achieve certainty in metaphysics by use of "the geometrical method." Developed a pantheism in which God and Nature are identical. Held a double-aspect theory of the mind-body problem. English translation: *Ethics*, 1883.

Sunya See Sunyavada.

Sunyavada   Madhyamika Buddhist philosophy holding that ultimate reality, *sunya* (void), is void of distinctions. *Sunya* is not different from "suchness," the way things appear in everyday experience. What is without distinction cannot be described; but the traditional Buddhist principle of fourfold negation may be used to describe the undescribable nature of each thing: A tree is neither temporal, nor nontemporal, nor both temporal and nontemporal, nor neither temporal nor nontemporal. See Nagarjuna.

Theravada Buddhism   Currently dominating philosophy of Hinayana Buddhism prevailing in Ceylon, Burma, Thailand, and Cambodia. Holds the doctrine that all is really impermanent, and that all beliefs about persisting things, selves, gods, or forms are mistaken. Attachment to things, and so on, as if permanent results from desire, which results from ignorance, both of which must be extinguished before freedom from illusion is possible.

Vallabha   (1481–1533)   Pantheistic critic of Shankara who is also nondualistic (advaita) but who accepts *Saguna Brahman* as the ultimate reality.

Vedantists   See Advaita Vedanta.

Whitehead, Alfred North   (1861–1947)   British philosopher who taught and wrote much of his philosophy after coming to the United States. He was a major process philosopher, holding that existence consists of "actual occasions" that happen but somehow incorporate relatedness to other things in the universe, past and future, into their momentary being. The forms of occasions are "eternal objects" which "ingress" when needed. God has both a "primordial" nature consisting of eternal objects and a "consequent nature" which interdepends with each actual occasion and thus is in process. Chief work: *Process and Reality*, 1929.

Zeno   (c. 490–430 B.C.)   Follower of Parmenides who argued against belief in the reality of change by formulating several paradoxes of motion.

INDEX

253